Sheila Durie and Rob Edw

Fuelling the Nuclear Arms Race

The Links between Nuclear Power and Nuclear Weapons

Pluto Press

Militarism, State and Society

Series editor: Dan Smith

Pluto's series on militarism, state and society will provide political analysis as well as new information and argument relating to current political controversies in the field of nuclear weapons, military policy and disarmament. It aims to present radical analyses and critiques of the existing orthodoxies in readable and accessible form.

First published 1982 by Pluto Press Limited,
Unit 10 Spencer Court, 7 Chalcot Road, London NW1 8LH

Copyright © Sheila Durie and Rob Edwards 1982

ISBN 0 86104 372 3

Cover designed by Clive Challis GrR
Cover illustration by Peter Kennard

Photoset in Great Britain by
Photobooks (Bristol) Limited
Barton Manor, St Philips, Bristol
Printed by Eyre & Spottiswoode Ltd., at Grosvenor Press, Portsmouth

Contents

Acknowledgements / 6
List of Abbreviations / 7
Introduction / 9
1. **The Birth of Siamese Twins** / 11
2. **The Nuclear Chain** / 31
3. **Atoms for Peace?** / 55
4. **Towards the Nuclear State** / 80
5. **Breaking the Nuclear Chain** / 98
   Appendix 1. Nuclear Power and Paths to the Bomb / 106
   Appendix 2. The Creation of Plutonium in Britain / 109
   Glossary of Technical Terms / 110
   Select Bibliography / 112
   References / 114
   Index / 128

Diagram: The Nuclear Fuel and Weapons Cycle / 32
Map: Nuclear Sites in Britain / 50

Acknowledgements

Many people have assisted us with the writing of this book. We owe a particular debt to Howard Clark, Robin Cook, Margaret Gowing and Nikki Ostrowski who were all invaluable in their different ways. We are also very grateful to Deirdre Armstrong, Don Arnott, Colin Booth, Peter Bunyard, James Daglish, Norman Dombey, Gari Donn, Kathleen and Aelwyn Edwards, Dave Elliott, Ian Fairlie, Michael Flood, Andy Follis, Martin Gaba, Jos Gallacher, Carol Graham, Alan Hines, Colin Holden, Mike Holderness, Claire Holman, David Jardine, Duncan Laxen, Amory Lovins, Bob Lowe, Walt Patterson, Ben Plumpton, Stan Reid, Fiona Riddoch, Pete Roche, Dave Rosenfeld, Paul Rowntree, Martin Ryle, Donald Scott, John Simpson, Dan Smith, David Somervell, Martin Stott, Mike Sweatman, Peter Taylor, Simon Taylor, Ian Welsh, Geoff Young and many others. Responsibility for the facts and arguments used is, of course, our own.

We dedicate the book to Andy and Fiona who sustained us separately.

Edinburgh
December 1981

Sheila Durie
Rob Edwards

List of Abbreviations

ABCC	Atomic Bomb Casualty Commission
AGR	Advanced Gas-cooled Reactor
AWRE	Atomic Weapons Research Establishment
BEA	British Electricity Authority
BNFL	British Nuclear Fuels Limited
BCUPD	British Civil Uranium Procurement Directorate
CDA	Combined Development Agency
CEGB	Central Electricity Generating Board
CND	Campaign for Nuclear Disarmament
Euratom	European Atomic Energy Community
FBI	Federal Bureau of Investigation
FBR	Fast Breeder Reactor
GE	General Electric (United States)
GEC	General Electric Company (Britain)
Hex	Uranium hexafluoride
IAEA	International Atomic Energy Agency
ICI	Imperial Chemical Industries Limited
ICRP	International Commission on Radiological Protection
INFCE	International Fuel Cycle Evaluation
LWR	Light Water Reactor
MinTech	Ministry of Technology (Britain)
MoD	Ministry of Defence (Britain)
MUF	Material Unaccounted For
NATO	North Atlantic Treaty Organisation
NPT	Nuclear Non-Proliferation Treaty
NRPB	National Radiological Protection Board
OPEC	Organisation of Petroleum Exporting Countries
PFR	Prototype Fast Reactor
PIPPA	Pressurised Pile for Producing Power and Plutonium
PWR	Pressurised Water Reactor
RTZ	Rio Tinto Zinc
SALT	Strategic Arms Limitation Talks
SSEB	South of Scotland Electricity Board
TNT	Tri-Nitro Toluene
UKAEA	United Kingdom Atomic Energy Authority
UN	United Nations
USAEC	United States Atomic Energy Commission

Human society is too diverse, national passion too strong, human aggressiveness too deep-seated for the peaceful and the warlike atom to stay divorced for long. We cannot embrace one while abhorring the other; we must learn, if we want to live at all, to live without both.

Jacques-Yves Cousteau, 1976

Introduction

In H.G. Wells's extraordinarily prescient novel about atomic energy, *The World Set Free*, published in 1914, the character who first demonstrates the potential for atomic bombs and atomic power has second thoughts. He notes in his diary: 'Felt like an imbecile who has presented a box full of loaded revolvers to a creche.'

On 12 December 1979, NATO, zealously supported by the British government, decided to deploy 572 new American nuclear missiles in Europe. Of these, 160 Tomahawk ground-launched cruise missiles are due, from 1983, to be sited in Britain at Greenham Common near Newbury and at Molesworth near Huntingdon. Six days later, on 18 December, the Secretary of State for Energy, David Howell, announced that the government considered it a 'reasonable prospect' to plan on ordering 'at least one new nuclear power station a year in the decade from 1982', the first of which is destined for Sizewell in Suffolk. Finally, on 24 January 1980, the House of Commons backed the government's intention to maintain an independent strategic nuclear force by replacing the Polaris missile system with Trident, a decision that could mean over 2,000 new nuclear warheads for Britain.

Within less than fifty days, then, the Conservative government had committed Britain to a massive escalation in both nuclear arms and nuclear power stations. The purpose of this book is – for the first time – to explore in depth how these momentous decisions are related.

Public understanding of the connections between nuclear power and nuclear weapons is limited. The nuclear industry's propaganda does not help by obscuring facts behind a smokescreen of misinformation. We have set out to distinguish myth from fact and to provide as complete and as honest a picture as possible of the strands that bind civil and military nuclear activities.

In Chapter 1 we chart the technical and institutional history of the development and use of atomic energy in Britain up to the present day, focusing in a way that has not been done before on the interplay between civil and military. Chapter 2 deals firstly with all the major nuclear installations now in Britain site by site, examining the civil and military use of each establishment. It carries on to outline some more general related topics and finishes with a close look at the nuclear links between Britain and the United States. Chapter 3 describes the international proliferation of nuclear weapons and how it is related to the spread of nuclear power. Chapter 4 looks at the secrecy that surrounds nuclear issues in Britain and examines the implications for civil liberties of nuclear expansion. Finally, in Chapter 5 we draw together our conclusions, briefly criticising the alleged 'need' for nuclear power, and spell out the policies that we believe must flow from our analysis.

A major problem in writing and reading about nuclear issues is the degree of technical understanding and literacy that is assumed. As a general rule we have tried to minimise the use of opaque jargon. Where unusual terms have been necessary we give a very simple explanatory description on their first use in the text, and also provide a glossary of technical terms on pages 110-11. Readers unfamiliar with the basic processes that make up the nuclear fuel and weapons cycle would find it helpful to refer to Appendix 1, *Nuclear Power and Paths to the Bomb*, where we explain in simple terms the relevant physics and technology. We use the terms 'nuclear' and 'atomic' more or less interchangeably, although 'atomic' is the more usual adjective for the early years of development. The 'atomic project' or 'atomic energy project' mean the early joint weapons *and* electricity project, whereas terms like 'atomic power' and 'nuclear power' refer to the electricity-producing uses of the atom. Appendix 2 deals with the problem of how much plutonium has in fact been created in Britain.

For readers anxious to pursue some of the issues raised we provide a select bibliography on pages 112-13. Our knowledge and understanding of the precise relationship between nuclear power and weapons is constantly being refined in the light of new information. If any readers feel they can assist us in that process, we would be glad to hear from them.

1.

The Birth of Siamese Twins

The development of nuclear power and nuclear weapons has been like that of Siamese twins. Joined physically at birth, they have grown up together and pushed and pulled each other into shape. At each stage, military criteria have determined civil progress and moulded the technological and institutional character of civil developments. Many of the civil programme's economic problems can be traced back to military decisions. Nuclear power is a spin-off from war-time efforts to develop atomic bombs: it may never have surfaced or survived on its own.

Although studies of atomic structure and the physical properties of the element uranium had been undertaken at various points up to the twentieth century, the crucial discoveries were made at the end of the 1930s. The timing was vitally important: the world was on the brink of war. While the scientific community was buzzing with the news of Joliot-Curie's experiments showing the possibility of a chain reaction, politicians were contemplating Hitler's rise to military power. 1939 saw a quantum leap in knowledge, as scientists recognised that splitting the atom would generate vast amounts of energy, in accordance with Einstein's famous equation $e=mc^2$ (energy is equivalent to mass times the speed of light squared). There was an international flurry of research in the months before war was declared.[1]

The possibility of making a bomb using the newly-discovered principles of atomic fission was immediately recognised. The chances of producing one, however, seemed slim. Had it not been for the impetus of war, and the fear that Nazi Germany would be making such a weapon, the whole course of atomic energy development might well have been different. The war-time leader of the US atomic bomb programme, General Groves, has said that the project would never have been undertaken in times of peace – the costs and difficulties would have been too great.[2]

Britain was the first country to take seriously the possibility of making atomic bombs. In 1940, the scientists Peierls and Frisch outlined how a bomb of manageable size could be made from pure uranium 235 (a rare form of natural uranium), and their paper prompted the setting up in Britain of the top secret 'Maud Committee' in April 1940.

The committee's scientists were to examine whether a bomb could be made, and if so, how. Scepticism was almost universal, but eighteen months' intensive work changed the situation completely. During their research, the Maud scientists also considered the possibility that atomic fission could be controlled and used to generate heat and electric power in a 'reactor'.

The Maud Committee reported in 1941, in two parts, considering both the bomb and reactor projects. Its findings confirmed that a bomb using uranium 235 could be made, but that separating enough of this material from natural uranium would be difficult. The reactor project was considered mainly in terms of its possible post-war industrial benefits, although the committee did think it relevant to the bomb project. The scientists' work had identified a new element, later named plutonium, which would be produced in a reactor, and which was rightly thought to be fissile and so usable in a bomb. The committee therefore recommended that although the bomb and reactor were two separate projects, 'their future must be considered together'.[3] Imperial Chemical Industries Ltd (ICI), involved in the atomic project from an early stage, added:

> There must always be a very close relationship between the exploitation of nuclear energy for military explosive purposes and for power production in peace and war. The development of one will have a profound effect on the development of the other.[4]

ICI in fact launched a bid to control the development of atomic power, which failed when responsibility for the project was transferred in 1941 from the Ministry of Aircraft Production to a new organisation within the government Department of Scientific and Industrial Research. Secrecy was extremely strict –

not even the whole war cabinet knew of the project's existence. Like the Maud Committee, the new organisation was given an innocuous cover-name: Tube Alloys. An ICI executive, Sir John Anderson, was given ministerial responsibility for the project.

Over the period of the Maud Committee, intensity of discussion and unity of purpose had combined to give Britain pre-eminence in atomic research. In 1942-43, however, after seeing the Maud Report, the US developed its own atomic project with astonishing rapidity, while the British merely marked time. With vast resources of money, materials and people, US research advanced on many fronts. Britain was eventually forced to accept a subordinate position, and limited collaboration was agreed upon in 1943, with the signing of the Quebec Agreement by the US, Britain and Canada. Work in Britain practically ceased, as scientists were transferred to the US atomic project – codenamed 'Manhattan' – where they gained much experience that was to prove vital in the development of Britain's post-war atomic project.

British scientists at Oak Ridge, the US enrichment plant (for increasing the proportion of uranium 235 atoms in natural uranium), later used some of their technical expertise in the design and construction of Britain's own enrichment plant at Capenhurst. Many British scientists went to Los Alamos in New Mexico and, under the direction of J. Robert Oppenheimer, acquired a comprehensive understanding of bomb construction. Key aspects of Britain's nuclear power industry, such as the design of reactors (also known as 'piles') and reprocessing (separating plutonium from the 'waste' from an atomic pile), came to be based on the Manhattan Project work carried out at the Montreal and Chalk River Laboratories in Canada.

Bombs or power?

The Future Systems Group at the Canadian laboratories attempted to develop designs for future piles, but encountered a dilemma. One design would maximise the yield of plutonium for bombs, while another would increase the efficiency of electricity generation. The military and industrial uses of atomic reactors appeared to be in conflict.

At the end of the war, this dilemma had not been resolved: no clear decision had been taken in Britain about developing either atomic bombs or power, but it was assumed by those involved that a British bomb would be made. The technical committee of Tube Alloys had met in 1944 to advise its minister, Sir John Anderson, on the shape of the atomic project, and recommended a programme which would produce ten bombs in the shortest possible time.

Atomic bomb manufacture required the large-scale production of either uranium 235 or plutonium 239. The US had huge resources and could afford to investigate all the options, but Britain was trying to recover from an exhausting war, and had to make an immediate choice between uranium and plutonium. The possibilities for developing atomic power depended on which material was chosen. Some senior scientific opinion favoured following the uranium route to bombs, but the military advantages of plutonium won the argument. Plutonium was a much more efficient and compact explosive, likely to be cheaper to produce. The creation of plutonium in atomic piles also solved the dilemma of whether to go for bombs or power, as it emerged that the process could be developed to make both.

The size of any atomic programme would be determined by how many bombs could actually be produced. One pile was thought to be capable of producing enough plutonium for fifteen bombs a year.[5] The government had no policy on the place of atomic bombs within defence strategy: they were largely symbolic of a lingering belief in British greatness. In December 1945, a meeting of seven cabinet ministers under the newly-elected Attlee government decided to build one pile as a matter of urgency. A month later, the military Chiefs of Staff outlined the philosophy of deterrence, and said that the output of one pile would be insignificant – the strength of the policy lay in numbers – and a second pile was authorised. The government also authorised a gas diffusion enrichment plant to enrich the fuel for the plutonium-producing piles,[6] although this was not begun until 1949.

The organisation was then brought together under Lord Portal, a former Chief of Air Staff, to carry out the work. It was split into three, according to its main functions: general research at Harwell in Oxfordshire, production at Risley near Warrington and weapons research and assembly, later housed at Aldermaston near Reading. The two men chosen to run Harwell and

Aldermaston – John Cockcroft and William Penney respectively – had been prominent in the Manhattan Project. Christopher Hinton, who took charge of Risley, was a top ICI engineer who had been responsible for government ordnance factories during the war.

Harwell: For many years, Harwell symbolised atomic energy in the public mind. It was at the forefront of science, accorded special privileges,[7] and developing what was seen as the most promising discovery of the century. Scientists were drawn to work there by the reputation of John Cockcroft, who took charge in January 1946, and by a sense of idealism – a desire to demonstrate that the atom could be used for peace as well as war and hope that atomic power could rid the world of pollution caused by coal.

In fact, Harwell's main task was to advance weapons-related research. Although most scientists were not anxious to work on the bomb, they held no strong feelings against it, while Cockcroft gave the impression that work on the bomb would be minimal, even though he firmly believed that 'a large nuclear power development was important in raising the British military potential'.[8] About forty per cent of the scientists at Harwell had in fact been with the Manhattan Project.

Risley: Christopher Hinton was given responsibility for coordinating the design, construction and operation of the facilities to produce plutonium in February 1946, a month after Cockcroft. Though remarkably few new processes emerged in the development of atomic energy, the sheer scale and urgency of the project made Hinton's task formidable.[9] From 1946 up to the British atomic bomb test in 1952, Hinton's team of designers and engineers at Risley constructed two atomic piles and a reprocessing plant at Windscale, a uranium metal fuel fabrication plant at Springfields and an enrichment plant at Capenhurst. These facilities, built to provide the material for Britain's atomic bombs, formed the foundation of the subsequent 'civil' nuclear power programme.

Aldermaston: The actual construction of an atomic bomb – the job to be done at Aldermaston – did not go ahead until the government gave formal authorisation in 1947. This decision, like that to build the first atomic pile, was not made as part of any coherent military strategy. According to the atomic project's official historian, Professor Margaret Gowing, it 'emerged' from 'general feelings of British greatness'.[10]

The public image of atomic energy

The public did not realise the extent of military domination of atomic energy: denied knowledge about the work at Aldermaston and Risley, it was the Harwell image of pure science that was portrayed in the media. There were very few press references to atomic bomb production, most articles referring to plutonium as 'atomic power material'. Parliament was also kept in relative ignorance. In the whole period of the Labour government (1945-51), there was not one House of Commons debate on atomic energy, for which MPs must bear some blame.[11] The only indication to parliament that anything was being done came in May 1948, when the Defence Minister, A.V. Alexander, revealed:

> Research and development continue to receive the highest priority in the defence field, and all types of modern weapons, including atomic weapons, are being developed.[12]

The announcement was pre-arranged, and made only to free channels of communication on the atomic project between government departments. Strangely, it was covered by a 'D Notice', the voluntary ban on publication adopted by the press on matters indicated by government as being too sensitive to publish. The press adhered fairly consistently to the ban.

The financing of the atomic project was also kept a close secret. When responsibility for the project was transferred from the Department of Scientific Research to the Ministry of Supply in 1945, the finance estimates were, according to Gowing, 'concealed from parliament by burying them in sub-headings of the Ministry of Supply vote'.[13] When Winston Churchill took office in 1951, he expressed some sarcastic admiration that Labour had managed to hide the £100 million (in 1951 prices) spent on atomic energy.[14]

Secrecy also surrounded the staff at atomic energy establishments, who were not allowed to talk about their work. The existence of Aldermaston was not publicly acknowledged until

1953. Security measures tightened after the conviction of a few nuclear scientists, notably Klaus Fuchs, as Russian spies.

British and US collaboration over the development of the post-war atomic project ceased in 1946 with the passing of the MacMahon Act in the US,[15] and was not to begin again until after Russia's atomic test in 1949. These years of separate development meant that Britain, developing the kind of pile first thought of at Montreal, started on the lonely path that led to the Magnox and advanced gas-cooled reactors, while the US developed light water reactors (LWRs). By giving heavy subsidies to countries that wished to build LWRs,[16] the US came to dominate world reactor markets, and Britain was unable to gain any significant export market for its reactors.

The British bomb

By 1947, Cockcroft, Hinton and Penney had settled down to produce a British atomic bomb. Hinton's team began work on 'Britain's atomic factories'.[17] At Springfields near Preston, uranium oxide was to be converted into pure uranium metal and then fabricated into fuel for the plutonium production piles. Construction began in 1948 and the first bars of uranium metal were cast in October of that year. In 1947, site clearance began at a royal ordnance factory at Windscale in Cumbria, and construction of the two piles began a mere two months later. Another stage in the fuel cycle, reprocessing, began operation there in 1950. Another old ordnance factory at Capenhurst near Chester was taken over in 1949 for the construction of a plant providing a small degree of enrichment of the fuel for the Windscale piles. A plant to provide highly-enriched uranium to be used directly in atomic weapons was authorised in 1951, and began low-level production in 1957.

The air-cooled design of the first Windscale piles was inefficient and costly: the heat produced was wasted, and each pile required blowers to circulate the air which consumed £340,000 worth of electricity per annum (1951 prices).[18] Hinton thought the design could be much improved, and was working on a design using gas under pressure as the coolant which would generate electricity. When he put forward a plan to alter the second pile along these lines, Lord Portal curtly rejected it:

> I would be much happier if I felt that the whole of the production side under me was animated by a single purpose, namely to produce fissile material in substantial quantities at the earliest possible date.[19]

As Professor Gowing comments: 'Military needs had given atomic energy its big push forwards, but now they were twisting its development'.[20]

At the beginning of 1948, the scale of atomic energy production was reviewed in the light of defence requirements. Although the two Windscale piles might provide something under a hundred bombs by 1957, the Chiefs of Staff wanted more than double that. The review, for virtually the first time, posed the question of whether Britain should be making bombs at all. Lord Portal, however, successfully argued that the abandonment of bombs would not save any money, as it would still be necessary to develop atomic energy for industrial use. Atomic power was now being used as a justification for the development of atomic weapons.

The first Windscale pile began operating in October 1950, the second in June 1951. The first plutonium was extracted by the Windscale reprocessing plant in February 1952, and sent to Aldermaston in August that year for incorporation into Britain's first atomic bomb. On 3 October 1952 the bomb was tested at Monte Bello, off the northern coast of Australia.

The Monte Bello test marked a change in atomic objectives. The comparatively small effort hitherto devoted to developing atomic energy to produce electricity began to increase, although for many years the bulk of research and production was still in support of the weapons programme. Accompanying the slight shift in direction was a change in the language: the word 'atomic' was replaced by 'nuclear'.

Further military demands

When Harwell first presented proposals for a nuclear power programme in 1949, it favoured the fast breeder reactor (FBR) – a reactor designed to create plutonium for use as fuel, to economise on uranium which was in short supply at the time. The FBR, however, conflicted with military objectives, and hence was not vigorously pursued.

At the 1950 Harwell Power Conference, the engineer R.V. Moore attempted the first serious analysis of nuclear power costs. He reckoned that natural uranium reactors would be economically competitive with electricity from coal stations at irradiations (i.e. the length of time the fuel spends in the reactor) that were much lower than previous estimates. The prospect of an economic nuclear power programme was now considered reasonable, though as Professor Gowing notes, 'the comparatively low limits of economic irradiation had another important consequence: they were low enough for the military production of plutonium'.[21]

Harwell meanwhile had developed their natural uranium design into something called PIPPA: pressurised pile for producing power and plutonium. Although harbouring doubts about its potential, Harwell asked the British Electricity Authority early in 1952 to cooperate in the design of a 10 megawatt prototype. The stage seemed set for the cautious development of nuclear power via the small-scale PIPPA. But at the end of 1952, the pace and path of development was radically altered.

The Chiefs of Staff had reviewed their atomic weapons policies and decided to develop a strategic air offensive capability. As in 1948, they calculated that more bombs would be needed, and demanded that plutonium production be doubled over the next three years.

Building another Windscale pile to meet this demand was considered too expensive, and besides, as one senior nuclear enthusiast Lord Cherwell argued, 'power production would have a good psychological effect on public opinion'.[22] PIPPA was thus developed from a small feasibility study to a large project for two full-scale piles producing plutonium, with power as a by-product.

If it had not been for the Chiefs of Staffs' demands for more plutonium, it is conceivable that PIPPA would have been mothballed in favour of reactors using different materials – the heavy water reactor or the helium-cooled high temperature reactor – or eventually the FBR. As it was, Risley's work on the FBR was abandoned in order to rapidly design a full-scale PIPPA. Thus the choice of natural uranium gas-cooled reactors was crystallised through military necessity, but at a pace none of those involved in the atomic project had foreseen, or advocated. Professor Gowing sums it up:

> Without the demand for military plutonium, a different kind of power reactor might have been developed. But without that demand, it is unlikely that government would have financed so soon two big prototype reactors and unlikely therefore that Britain could or would have launched a large-scale nuclear programme as early as the mid-fifties.[23]

Calder Hall and Chapelcross: In January 1953, the Minister of Supply, Duncan Sandys, announced that a 100 megawatt, twin reactor, power station named Calder Hall would be built adjacent to the Windscale site. In 1955, with construction of the two reactors at Calder Hall well under way, the Ministry of Fuel and Power announced that a further two were to be built at the site. Shortly afterwards, a second station of four reactors was announced, to be built at Chapelcross in Dumfriesshire. The Chapelcross design was identical to Calder Hall, and was also primarily a plutonium producer for the military, generating electricity as a by-product.

To date, Calder Hall and Chapelcross have been the only British nuclear power stations to be built to time. Calder Hall was opened by the Queen on 17 October 1956, in a blaze of publicity. *The Times* ran a sixteen page supplement, and guests from the atomic industries worldwide were present to celebrate the event. Calder Hall was hailed as 'the world's first nuclear power station', but its prime role in producing British bombs was not mentioned. The Queen's speech was the epitome of 'Atoms for Peace' hypocrisy:

> Future generations will judge us, above all else by the way in which we use these limitless opportunities which Providence has given us . . . They offer us . . . a vital and timely addition to the industrial resources of our nation . . . we have something new to offer to the people of the undeveloped and less fortunate areas of the world . . . It may well prove to have been among the greatest of our contributions to human welfare that we led the way in demonstrating the peaceful uses of this new source of power.[24]

The greatest of Calder Hall's contributions, at least until the mid-

1960s, was not to human welfare but to warfare. By 1964, a well.informed commentator put Britain's nuclear weapons stockpile at 1,000-1,500 weapons.[25] It is impossible to assess accurately, but this first 'power station' seems likely to have contributed the plutonium for about a quarter of this number.[26]

The birth of the UKAEA

With the first British atomic test, and the decision to build Calder Hall, came renewed debate on the proper organisation and control of the atomic project: the very scale of activity demanded some re-organisation. Since 1951, Lord Cherwell had been promoting the idea of an independent corporation – a semi-governmental body similar to the US Atomic Energy Commission. In 1953, Prime Minister Churchill set up a committee under Sir John Anderson to plan a transfer of responsibility to such a corporation. A Bill embodying the committee's recommendations was presented to parliament in February 1954, and the United Kingdom Atomic Energy Authority (UKAEA) came into existence on 19 July of that year.

Rather than allow full parliamentary control of atomic energy, the UKAEA was set up as a semi-autonomous non-departmental body under ministerial control, and thus accorded a special place within government. By transferring responsibility to a non-departmental minister (the Lord President of the Council), the government hoped to be in 'a very much better position to assess the balance between the civil and military uses of what is the same material'.[27]

The UKAEA administered both civil and military nuclear development, ensuring that the atomic twins were not separated. Nor could they be at this stage: of the atomic work carried out so far, according to the government, 'weapons were nine-tenths of the total'.[28] As the UKAEA's chairman from 1967-81, Sir John Hill, has observed:

> The entire nuclear defence programme and the embryo civil nuclear power programme lay in the establishments of the UKAEA . . . The facilities required for the manufacture and reprocessing of the nuclear fuel . . . were virtually identical to those required for the defence programme.[29]

The UKAEA inherited all the facilities built for the production of atomic weapons, including Aldermaston, and had an initial payroll of 17,000. Its capital assets from the bomb programme amounted to £154.7 million in 1954 prices,[30] equivalent to a staggering subsidy of over £1 billion in 1981 prices. The total eventual subsidy was probably higher: Gowing quotes a figure of £160 million up to 1953,[31] all spent without any parliamentary scrutiny. As there seemed little hope in 1954 of making atomic energy pay its way, the UKAEA was financed by parliamentary vote. The UKAEA's budget was not determined by comparison with spending on other energy research, but simply in accordance with its own demands, by preparing its estimates for the forthcoming year which parliament merely rubber-stamped. By 1959, the UKAEA had assets of £450 million, and was spending over £100 million of taxpayers' money per year (1959 prices).[32]

The 'old boy' network

The UKAEA retained the three groups of the post-war organisation (research and development, production and weapons), and many of the same top scientists and administrators. Top positions in the early development of nuclear power were given to people previously involved in the military project. Cockcroft, Hinton and Penney became board members, and the latter was UKAEA Chairman from 1964-67. Senior scientists from the military project also moved into the government departments concerned with atomic power in the 1950s and 1960s. These people made up a powerful group with shared experience, ideas and goals.[33]

In 1957, Christopher Hinton was transferred to the Central Electricity Generating Board (CEGB) to effect the commercial establishment of the technology of which he had been the chief architect. Ten days after the UKAEA came into existence, the Lord President had directed that the production of power from nuclear energy on a commercial basis was to be carried out by the electricity authorities, then the British Electricity Authority (BEA), with the UKAEA giving advice and training. But the relationship was uncomfortable. The UKAEA was the policy developer, not the BEA or its successors. The electricity boards were made responsible for the first nuclear power programme in 1955 without having any say in the decision-making, and only having 'a month or so' to comment on the draft.[34]

The third partner in the development of nuclear power was private industry, though playing a more subordinate role than their counterparts in the US. On the advice of the UKAEA, private firms were organised into consortia, with the overall responsibility for design and construction resting with Risley. A number of the firms had already undertaken work for the Risley organisation, but because of the secrecy surrounding the atomic project, industrial development problems had mainly been hidden. According to Gowing again:

> Private industry had, before the first British bomb test in 1952, shown little enthusiasm for atomic energy but before long was clamouring for entry. Since secrecy had concealed the magnitude and complexity of the difficulties, firms saw only the successful industrial outcome and painful disillusion was to lie ahead.[35]

The 'painful disillusion' was illustrated by the reduction by merger of the consortia from five to three in 1960, the collapse of another consortium in 1969 and the eventual creation in 1973 of a single design and construction company, the National Nuclear Corporation, in which the companies became shareholders.[36]

The 1955 White Paper 'A programme of nuclear power' stated that 'the military programme continues to be of great importance but the peaceful applications of nuclear energy now demand attention'.[37] Three stages were envisaged: the first four stations were to be based on an improved version of the Calder Hall design, later to be called 'Magnox' after the name of the alloy surrounding the uranium fuel: the next four might be similar, but of a more advanced design; while the last four might be liquid-cooled reactors. It was hoped that the next decade would see the establishment of FBRs. In total, 1,500-2,000 megawatts were to be built between 1960 and 1965 and operated by the CEGB. The programme was given a massive subsidy because, as the White Paper states, 'the present ancillary plant, which has been built and is primarily used for military purposes, will be adequate at first for a commercial programme of this size'. "Ancillary plant" means the capital assets represented by Windscale, Springfields and Capenhurst.

The official justification of the nuclear power programme based on Magnox reactors was not that nuclear power was economically comparable with conventional generation (by coal and oil), but that a gap was expected to open up between Britain's energy requirements and the availability of fuel, mainly coal. Nevertheless, it was the government's belief, advised by the UKAEA, that nuclear power would be roughly competitive.

Following the 1956 Suez crisis, there was considerable concern over the reliability of oil supplies. This was a major factor in prompting the announcement in March 1957 of a trebling of the programme based on Magnox reactors: 5,000-6,000 megawatts of nuclear capacity were to be built by 1965. Inspired perhaps by Hinton's important lecture in Stockholm in 1957, which optimistically predicted that Magnox-generated electricity would be economically competitive by 1962-63, the British government committed itself to producing relatively more nuclear electricity than any other country in the world. But even before the first Magnox stations were ordered, the economics of nuclear power had begun to deteriorate.

One of the main reasons for this was a dramatic fall in the so-called 'plutonium credit', which was calculated as a reduction in the estimated cost of generating electricity, and which had nothing to do with the military.[38] It had been hoped that plutonium from the early Magnox reactors could be used to fuel the next generation of reactors, but by the late 1950s it was realised that plutonium could only be used in the FBRs, which seemed a long way off. Secondly, supplies of uranium became more plentiful and prices dropped, as new mines entered full production in many countries. Thirdly, the US Atomic Energy Commission (USAEC) cut its price for enriched uranium by more than one third in 1956. Thus there was no longer any need to eke out uranium supplies by burning plutonium. As a result, in 1963 the plutonium credit fell to zero.

By June 1960, and the second White Paper on the nuclear power programme, it was recognised that the previous hopes for an economic Magnox programme were unfounded. Interest rates had risen, affecting capital-intensive nuclear stations more than conventional ones, and there had been a dramatic drop in the costs of conventional plant as efficiency had increased. Electricity from the first Magnox station, finished in 1962, cost 80 per cent more than was estimated in 1957.[39] By 1960, the CEGB were pressing for reductions in the programme. In the

1960 White Paper, the government recognised that conventional electricity generation was 25 per cent cheaper than nuclear generation.[40]

The Magnox stations have also been beset by technical difficulties. In 1969 it was discovered that they all had unexpected corrosion problems, and their output was restricted by between 10-20 per cent. The effect on generating costs was disguised by lowering the reactors' generating capacity from the originally specified level, thereby artificially maintaining their operating efficiency. Since 1979, cracks have been discovered in the cooling system of four Magnox stations and others, notably the latest and largest, have low load factors resulting from accidents and other technical difficulties.

Far from being the 'workhorses' of the electricity supply system as the electricity boards claim, the Magnox reactors have proved an expensive failure. The military influence on the development of nuclear power precipitated the choice of a reactor system that was too undeveloped to form the basis of a commercial power programme, and which has imposed a severe financial burden on the taxpayer and electricity consumer.

The 1957 Windscale accident

During the setting up of the civil programme, the two Windscale piles kept on producing plutonium for Britain's expanding nuclear weapons arsenal. In 1957, Britain's most serious nuclear accident to date occurred in the no. 1 plutonium pile.[41] On 7 October, the pile was shut down for a fuel change and some routine adjustments. Three days later, it was realised that the fuel was on fire, with radioactive air discharging from the stack. Water was pumped in and the fire brought under control, but the problem of radioactivity remained. For the next six weeks, all milk produced in the surrounding 600 farms was poured into the sea – a total of 3 million gallons. Eventually, the no. 1 pile was found to be completely unserviceable, and the no. 2 pile also had to be shut down because of the prohibitive cost of design changes to make it safe. This unexpected accident meant there would be a 'hiccup' in supplies of plutonium for weapons. In what *The Times* of 18 October 1957 described as a 'hastily arranged' meeting with Prime Minister Macmillan, the Chairman of the UKAEA and the Permanent Secretary at the Ministry of Defence, President

Eisenhower agreed to urge the US Congress to amend the MacMahon Act and permit resources to be pooled for the development of nuclear weapons.

In June 1958 it was announced that the CEGB had been asked to modify the design of three Magnox power stations to allow weapons-grade plutonium to be obtained from them.[42] A year later, the government said that only one station, Hinkley Point A, would in fact be modified.[43] The nature of the modifications was not specified at the time, but it has since been confirmed that they involved design changes to the machinery which refuels the reactor.[44] This would presumably be to allow the fuel to be changed more often, thereby producing plutonium with high proportions of plutonium 239 – the preferred isotope for bomb material – and at the same time preventing the build-up of plutonium 240 which is less stable and therefore less suitable for making weapons. (In fact it is now well established that plutonium with relatively high proportions of plutonium 240 can be used in nuclear weapons, and in any case, the refuelling of Magnox stations can be manipulated to produce 'weapons-grade' plutonium.[45]) The modifications were described by the government as 'a most valuable insurance against future possible defence requirements' which were said not to affect the cost of producing electricity.[46] This was disputed by *The Economist*, which stated that the process was 'grossly uneconomic'.[47]

In 1978 R.F. Pocock – a former nuclear engineer – revealed that problems with the modified refuelling machine caused construction delays.[48] It was not clear whether any use was actually made of the modifications until 1981 when the government stated that 'notwithstanding this limited contingency arrangement, Hinkley Point A has not in fact been operated in order to produce military-grade plutonium'.[49] What constitutes 'military-grade' plutonium is a matter of interpretation – any plutonium created in a Magnox reactor could conceivably be usable in weapons, either on its own or mixed with 'purer' grades of plutonium. There is a great deal of evidence that plutonium from Britain's supposedly civil Magnox power stations has in fact been used in nuclear weapons, as we shall see in Chapter 2.

Changes in the industry after 1960

In the period 1960-64, a major reshuffle of the defence

requirement for fissile material took place as a result of agreements with the US and greater reliance on hydrogen bombs. This had a marked effect on the UKAEA as, according to their 1960-61 Annual Report, a 'substantial proportion' of its effort was still 'devoted to the nuclear weapons programme as directed by the Ministry of Defence'.[50]

The Capenhurst enrichment plant to produce weapons-grade uranium came into full production in 1960, but almost immediately began to be run down. Production began decreasing in July 1962, and from 1963 the plant was kept operating at the lowest possible level. By 1964, the number of UKAEA employees had fallen by 5,000, a decrease which 'raised considerable problems for the Authority'.[51] Both the UKAEA in general and Aldermaston in particular were now given contracts of a non-nuclear nature. Aldermaston also took over work on the FBR.[52] The 1964 Statement on Defence announced that:

> supplies of fissile material already available or assured will be sufficient to maintain our independent deterrent and to meet all our defence requirements in the foreseeable future.

It added that military plutonium and uranium production was being ended, but that production could be 'resumed or increased' should the need arise.[53]

Since there were no plans to build further plutonium-producing piles, one wonders from where the capacity to 'resume or increase production' was going to come. Certainly Chapelcross, Calder Hall and Capenhurst could meet requirements at the previous level, but any increase would have to originate from the civil programme. Thus the 'insurance policy' of the Hinkley Point modification and the use of plutonium briefly irradiated in the Magnox stations may have been meant in this context.

The 'atomic factories' began to be organised primarily to deal with the civil fuel cycle, although the new reprocessing plant being built at Windscale was quoted as being 'mainly' (i.e. not exclusively) for civil use.[54] As the UKAEA, through the taxpayer, had borne the capital costs for the construction and operation of the facilities producing fissile material for the military, and as deliveries of their product would now be small, the arrangements for charging the MoD for fissile material had to be changed. It was therefore arranged that 'the Defence Departments will meet the outstanding capital liabilities by making eight annual payments from the Defence Budget to the AEA'.[55] The first payment was made in 1965, and the total subsidy to the UKAEA from this source amounted to £207 million.[56] Converting these payments into January 1981 prices gives an equivalent of about £720 million.[57]

As the military obligations of the UKAEA decreased in the 1960s, the industrial development of nuclear power took on its own momentum and status within government policy. As Britain's nuclear weapons plans stabilised, the 'push-me-pull-you' effect on nuclear power development waned, although the UKAEA still fulfilled defence requirements, maintaining the nuclear weapons arsenal using its dual-purpose facilities.

Between 1962-64, there was an intense debate over the type of reactor that should succeed the Magnox design.[58] The advanced gas-cooled reactor (AGR) – viewed as the logical successor to the Magnox – was adopted in 1965. From the outset, AGRs have been beset by major technical difficulties resulting in long construction delays. Out of five AGRs begun in the late 1960s, only two had been completed by mid-1981 – Hinkley Point B and Hunterston B – both of which have suffered expensive and unexpected accidents. Dungeness B, the first AGR to be ordered, was still awaiting completion in mid-1981. The cost of these delays has been enormous: in 1978, it was estimated that Dungeness B was costing more than double its original estimate of £89 million.[59] The economist Professor Duncan Burn estimated that the AGR programme had cost Britain £2,800 million more (in 1975 prices) than it would have cost to supply electricity from alternative sources.[60] By 1977, another economist, Professor David Henderson, was comparing the AGR programme with Concorde, as the greatest misallocation of public funds in British industrial history.[61] In 1981, Professor Burn updated his earlier estimates and put the cost to the taxpayer of the five AGRs at £11 billion (in January 1981 prices).[62]

The full and disastrous consequences of the Magnox and AGR programmes were understood too late. Decisions were taken in a military context by an industry still influenced by military demands, and as such were deeply secret and never open to effective public or parliamentary scrutiny. The UKAEA's special role as the developer of both technology and policy gave it enormous influence, especially as government ministers had no independent advice on nuclear matters.[63] It is likely that the nuclear industry would have encountered problems regardless of the type of reactor adopted. The military impetus given to nuclear power, and its potential for supporting the weapons programme, combined with sheer technological and institutional momentum to create a nuclear industry where none was really viable.

Organisational changes in the nuclear industry

In the 1970s, the structure of the British nuclear industry underwent two major institutional changes which, by design or default, have tended to obscure the basic historical links between nuclear power and nuclear weapons.

The first was the establishment of a new company, British Nuclear Fuels Ltd (BNFL). The setting up of a new organisation to handle the UKAEA's nuclear fuels business, hence leaving the UKAEA to concentrate more on research, was first mooted by the House of Commons Select Committee on Science and Technology in its 1967 report. BNFL came into being on 1 April 1971, and took over all the facilities that the military were using for the production of fissile material: Springfields, Capenhurst, Chapelcross, Calder Hall and, most important of all, Windscale. The financial basis for the transfer of these five large operations was, according to BNFL, obscure:

> Assets originally provided for defence purposes, and which the company may in certain circumstances be required to use for such purposes, had no value attributed to them on their transfer to the company.[64]

The government at the time made it clear that BNFL was expected to play an important military role:

> Many of the operations of the fuel company . . . are likely to be very sensitive from the point of view of national security. The company will be engaged in the enrichment of uranium and the separation of plutonium, as well as in the supply of fissile material for military purposes.[65]

The second change was the transfer of responsibility for the UKAEA Weapons Group to the Ministry of Defence in 1973.

Under the Atomic Energy Authority (Weapons Group) Act, the control and ownership of Aldermaston and its associated facilities, which had been with the UKAEA since its inception in 1954, passed to the Secretary of State for Defence. Section 6 of the Act modified the UKAEA's previous powers to research and develop nuclear weapons by prohibiting work on 'any nuclear explosive device, whether for war-like applications or otherwise, except in accordance with arrangements made with the Secretary of State'.[66] The Act also allows the UKAEA access to all the information it had previously owned in the Weapons Group on application to the Secretary of State, and enables the UKAEA to carry out, on request, work for the MoD. The effect has been to separate awareness in the public mind of Aldermaston – Britain's biggest nuclear weapons research establishment – and the UKAEA – the main pro-nuclear power protagonist in the 'public debate' on nuclear power.

In spite of appearances, however, the civil and military sides of the nuclear industry are still closely linked. Like Siamese twins grown up together, nuclear power and nuclear weapons can never be separated without one, or both, dying.

2.

The Nuclear Chain

Any attempt to map out the precise links in the civil and military nuclear chain is gravely hampered by secrecy. Parliamentary questions are unanswered or side-stepped, letters are brushed aside and sometimes ignored completely, and diligent research through pages of official reports is often unrewarding. There has been a deliberate attempt to separate the atomic bomb and nuclear electricity in the public mind, which has added to difficulties in obtaining reliable information. Yet, as the world lurches nearer nuclear war, the task of understanding and interpreting the existing specific relationships between nuclear power and weapons has never been more important.

The main villain of the piece is British Nuclear Fuels Ltd (BNFL). A glance at the company's annual reports, or a careful read of its many glossy brochures, leaves the average observer with a firm impression of BNFL as a nuclear fuel business solely devoted to assisting in the production of nuclear electricity. This is an extremely misleading picture: all of BNFL's establishments are dual purpose, all of them were predominantly military. The company has an extremely close relationship with the Ministry of Defence, and still operates some of Britain's key nuclear weapons plants: in the future its weapons-orientated work looks set to expand.

Windscale

The massive complex at Windscale on the Cumbrian coast is in many ways the centre of the intricate web that binds together civil and military. Its vital strategic importance is recognised by Britain's military planners: in the 1980 civil defence exercise 'Operation Square Leg' it was obliterated by an imaginary atom bomb.[1] All the plutonium for Britain's nuclear warheads has at one stage or another passed through Windscale. There is only

The Nuclear Fuel and Weapons Cycle

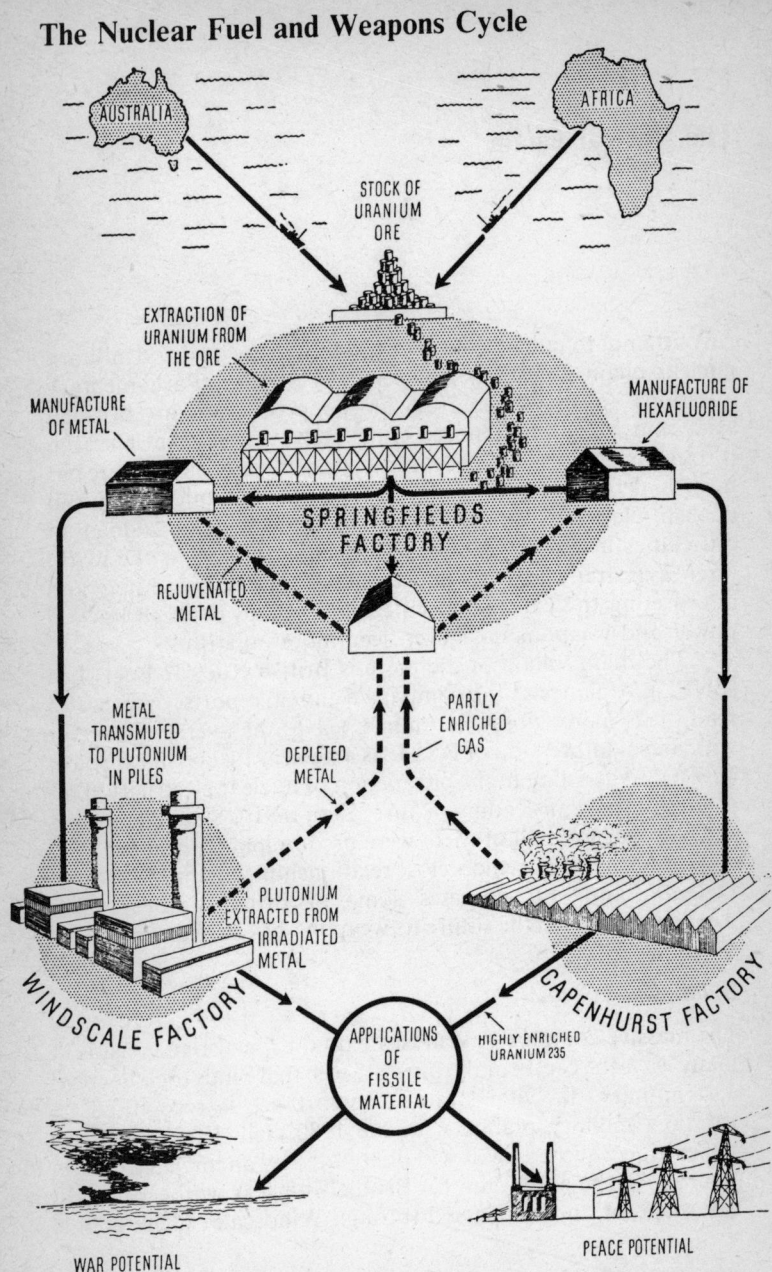

From: K. E. B. Jay, *Britain's Atomic Factories: The Story of Atomic Energy Production in Britain*, London, HMSO 1954. Reproduced with permission of the Controller of HMSO.

one major facility on the site with no definitely identifiable military function or potential – the UKAEA's experimental advanced gas-cooled reactor which was shut down in 1981.

Between 1950 and 1957 Britain's first two piles were run at Windscale, together producing enough plutonium for 30 atomic bombs a year.[2] Windscale's first reprocessing plant, named B204, was commissioned in 1952 and used, until it was closed in 1964, to extract plutonium from reactor spent fuel as part of the atomic bomb construction effort. The building was converted for the treatment of a different type of fuel, and operated as a preliminary separation plant, the purpose of which according to the UKAEA was 'mainly' – but not exclusively – civil.[3] This plant had to be shut down following an accident in 1973 when 35 workers were contaminated with radioactive ruthenium. The second reprocessing plant, B205, came into operation in 1964 and was also, according to BNFL, used for military purposes.[4] The proportion of civil work – producing plutonium for the fast reactor research programme and uranium for recycling in power reactors – is said to have increased during the 1970s. Each of the reprocessing plants is accompanied by an associated complex of facilities for treating spent fuel and separating out the plutonium, uranium and waste fission products.

Windscale also harbours Britain's only plutonium fuel fabrication plant, B277, which came into operation in 1969 to manufacture mixed plutonium/uranium oxide fuel elements for the prototype fast reactor at Dounreay. Although arguably a civil facility, as we shall see later the fast reactor fuel cycle has disturbing implications because of its dependence on plutonium that can be used in weapons.

During the 100-day Windscale Inquiry in 1977, some obscure allusions were made to a hitherto unacknowledged plant for 'plutonium recoveries'.[5] A witness for BNFL under cross-examination revealed that at least two-thirds of the hazardous plutonium and all the americium effluent from Windscale came from activities which he could not identify for security reasons. These activities were said to have been carried out in an annexe to the old reprocessing plant B204 and to consist of the recovery of 'aged plutonium residues'. Two observers have suggested that this small plant was and is used for the periodic reprocessing of nuclear warheads in order to remove plutonium decay-products which slowly build up and render weapons less predictable.[6] Although the government has said that 'in general' the reprocessing or replacement of fissile material in nuclear warheads is 'not necessary',[7] there is little doubt that warheads do require regular maintenance. Weapons ingredients do change and decay over time. In 1980 the Assistant Chief Scientific Adviser (Nuclear) at the Ministry of Defence, D.C. Fakley, told the House of Commons Defence Committee that all nuclear weapons had a finite life of between 10 and 20 years.[8]

Windscale also acts as a centre for the spent fuel from the pressurised water reactors that power Britain's four Polaris and growing number of 'hunter-killer' submarines (11 in 1981), and which are due to power Trident submarines. Although the quantities involved are secret, they are said not to be as great as the spent fuel arising from the much larger civil reactors. It appears that some spent fuel, such as that from the Rosyth naval dockyard in Fife, is stored at Windscale pending a decision on whether or not to reprocess it, while some has already been reprocessed and the resulting waste stored in one of Windscale's 15 highly-active waste storage tanks.[9] Plans for a special submarine spent fuel store at the site were revealed by the UKAEA in 1963.[10]

The eventual result of the Windscale Inquiry was that BNFL were given permission to build a large new oxide fuel reprocessing plant to deal with spent fuel from Britain's advanced gas-cooled reactors and from abroad. This was in spite of the fact that the expansion – which involved returning plutonium to the country of origin – was in conflict with US President Carter's initiatives to reduce the risks of international nuclear proliferation. The fear is that by separating and spreading more plutonium the plant could assist countries to acquire nuclear weapons capability. In 1981, the plant had still not been begun, but BNFL had announced another £100 million plan to build a 60-acre waste treatment complex including three plants, one for the storage and treatment of waste, one for the treatment of 'process residues' and a third as a 'development facility'. The government has admitted that this complex, which is not due to begin operation before 1990, may treat 'some residues arising from Ministry of Defence operations'.[11]

Since Windscale was first publicly identified as Britain's

'nuclear dustbin' in 1975, its public image has deteriorated to the point where in 1981 BNFL announced that the site was to be renamed 'Sellafield'.

Calder Hall

Adjacent to the Windscale site are the four 50 megawatt Calder Hall reactors, whose dishonest beginnings between 1956 and 1959 were outlined in Chapter 1. According to BNFL, the station, which produced a quarter of the plutonium for Britain's pre-1964 weapons programme, was modified between 1961 and 1967 and has been optimised for electricity production ever since.[12] It has a high – over 90 per cent – average load factor (a measure of operating efficiency) although reactor no. 1 was closed down between 1975 and 1981 to act as a store for a large backlog of spent Magnox fuel. The re-opening of reactor no.1 will of course help top up plutonium supplies.

Chapelcross

'Britain's new atomic explosives factory – which produces electricity as a bonus – is being officially opened today' proclaimed Scotland's *Daily Record* newspaper with unusual clarity on 2 May 1959 on the formal opening of the £34 million plant at Chapelcross near Annan in Dumfriesshire. Under the headline 'They'll carry H-bomb rods', the paper went on to explain how 'hand-picked' lorry drivers would ferry plutonium, 'the powerful atomic explosive', from Chapelcross to the 'explosives refinery' at Windscale. Chapelcross was set to 'turn out enough atomic explosive each year for a score of A-bombs or H-bomb triggers' and also, incidentally, to 'produce enough atomic electricity each year to meet the daily needs of a town of 70,000 people'.[13]

Chapelcross, run by BNFL, is a replica of Calder Hall, comprising four 50 megawatt reactors originally designed for the military but later 'optimised' for electricity production. Most people now regard the plant as a purely civil electricity producing power station, an illusion that is carefully encouraged by the industry. BNFL's glossy 1980 booklet on Chapelcross 'published as a contribution to the wider understanding of nuclear power' mentions not a word of the plant's predominantly military history. Indeed it says that the plutonium extracted from its spent fuel is simply 'stored for re-use as a fuel'.[14] In fact, certainly prior to 1964 and probably since then, the plutonium yielded by Chapelcross has gone into nuclear warheads. Perhaps even more disturbingly, there is no mention of what must be the single most important development at Chapelcross since the 1950s – the construction of a tritium separation plant.

Tritium is a radioactive isotope of hydrogen, and an essential component of the H-bomb. Like all radioactive materials it decays naturally, its activity decreasing by half about every twelve and a half years. Thus a continuous supply is necessary to enable its regular replacement in warheads. In April 1976 the Ministry of Defence announced that they had placed an order with BNFL for the supply of tritium, work that would involve the construction of a new plant. No cost for the project was, or ever has been, given, although it was expected to provide work for about fifty people.[15] The plant was completed early in 1980.

Tritium has no use in the electricity production process and does not occur naturally. It has to be manufactured by irradiating another element, lithium, in one of the Chapelcross reactors at the same time as it produces electricity. The irradiated lithium then has to be processed to extract the tritium – the task that required the new plant.[16]

Official pronouncements have said nothing more than that the plant is 'in aid of the United Kingdom nuclear weapons programme',[17] and that the decision to build it was based on 'sensible economic and practical grounds'.[18] Unofficially it is known that between 1959 and 1979, under a special defence agreement, Britain imported tritium for its H-bombs from the United States.[19] It seems likely that the decision to begin indigenous production at Chapelcross was linked to the ending of US supplies. Chapelcross is perceived and promoted as a civil power-producing establishment, yet in reality it houses one of Britain's most important military plants – a new source of 'fuel' for maintaining and augmenting the country's lethal arsenal of thermonuclear weapons.

Capenhurst

The role of BNFL's uranium enrichment establishment at Capenhurst in Cheshire has been as vital to weapons production as Windscale. The first plant built there in 1949 was a low enrichment 'gaseous diffusion' plant, to enrich the uranium discharged from the Windscale plutonium production piles so that it could be re-used as fuel in the piles. This was expanded by 1957 to enable it to enrich uranium to over 90 per cent for use either in atomic weapons or as fuel for the navy's nuclear-powered submarines. The plant began to be closed down in 1962, as the Ministry of Defence considered that its stockpile of highly enriched uranium, combined with imports from the United States under arrangements specified in a 1959 amended defence agreement, would ensure the supply of enough material for the weapons programme. We have seen no evidence that, since 1963, Capenhurst has been used to produce bombs-grade uranium. The military gaseous diffusion plant was refurbished in 1968 and started enriching uranium by just a few per cent for use in civilian advanced gas-cooled reactors. In 1981, it was announced that, due to public expenditure cuts, this plant would be closed 'earlier than had been planned', namely by the end of 1982.[20]

A new method for enriching uranium, the gas centrifuge, has also been developed at Capenhurst, with alarming military implications: the first such plant was commissioned in 1976, and a second is due to come into operation in 1982. These facilities are managed by an Anglo-Dutch-German collaborative venture called URENCO, in which BNFL has a third share. With gas centrifuge technology, unlike gaseous diffusion, it is possible to increase the number of enrichment stages simply by changing the plumbing connections, thereby making the adaption of low enrichment civil plants to high enrichment military purposes relatively easy and increasing the risks of proliferation.[21] When the technology was first mooted, the respected commentator Leonard Beaton argued in *The Times* that its introduction would mean that 'the problem of building hydrogen bombs would . . . be greatly simplified'.[22] Since the start of centrifuge work at Capenhurst and elsewhere such fears appear to have been justified. In 1980 a Dutch government inquiry concluded that 'facts justify the supposition' that Dr Abdul Khan – an employee in one of URENCO's other centrifuge plants at Almelo in Holland – stole secret plans for the construction of a centrifuge which were used to help Pakistan build an enrichment plant as part of the country's attempts to acquire nuclear weapons capability.[23]

One of URENCO's main deals, involving the supply of nearly four thousand tons of enriched uranium to Nuclebras of Brazil between 1981 and 1990, combined with nuclear reactors, an enrichment plant and a reprocessing plant from West Germany, could provide Brazil with atomic weapons. According to BNFL, the 1981 URENCO order book was worth £1,500 million, of which over a third was handled at Capenhurst.[24] Even BNFL Chairman Sir John Hill admitted in 1981 the risks of 'a technology that could be adapted for the production of weapons-grade uranium getting into the wrong hands'.[25]

Although the overtly military role of Capenhurst in the 1970s appears small, in the 1980s it is set to expand dramatically. In January 1980, the then Secretary of State for Defence, Francis Pym, announced that the Ministry of Defence was planning to build a new enrichment plant at the site 'to provide for the Royal Navy's long-term needs for fuel to be consumed in its nuclear propelled submarines'.[26] The plant was to be based on centrifuge technology and would provide 'the opportunity to resume indigenous production of highly-enriched uranium', which had been obtained from the gaseous diffusion plant until 1962 and since then from the US. Although the £100 million plant was originally due for completion in the mid-1980s, in 1981, work on it was delayed due to public expenditure cuts forcing the navy to economise.[27] The delay is presumably connected to the fact that in 1981 Britain was reported to have signed a new five-year contract with the US Department of Energy for the supply of highly-enriched uranium, ostensibly for nuclear submarine reactors.[28]

Fuel for submarine reactors, according to two seemingly reliable sources,[29] has to be enriched to over 90 per cent, a level that makes it indistinguishable from bombs-grade uranium. This has led some observers, like *The Times* Defence Correspondent Henry Stanhope, to argue that the plant was really designed to produce material for nuclear weapons.[30] Under the terms of the 1970 Almelo Agreement, which established URENCO, Britain is left free to use Capenhurst for weapons production, and according to the Netherlands government has apparently told its partners that it would be exercising this option.[31] Before the new plant was announced, nuclear analyst John Simpson speculated on the emergence of an enriched uranium 'bottleneck', and commented perceptively that restarting production of highly-enriched uranium 'may not have too many political penalties attached to it because it could be argued to be solely for the purposes of providing fuel for nuclear submarine reactors'.[32] Capenhurst's new defence-orientated plant could see the site's return to a central role in Britain's growing nuclear weapons industry.

Springfields

According to the UKAEA's first ever Annual Report in 1956, the Springfields fuel fabrication plant near Preston was completed in 1948 'to meet an urgent military requirement'.[33] It was built to fabricate uranium metal fuel for the two Windscale plutonium production piles, and for Calder Hall and Chapelcross. This relatively primitive plant has not been used since 1960, when it was replaced by a second facility which continued to make the fuel assemblies for Calder Hall and Chapelcross, as well as for the new generation of 'civil' Magnox reactors. In 1968, a plant for fabricating advanced gas-cooled reactor fuel was also brought into operation. Before uranium can be enriched, the ore has to be transformed into uranium hexafluoride, or 'hex' for short. This process is carried out at Springfields: the first hex conversion plant running between 1952 and 1968, when a second took over, both plants 'feeding' the various Capenhurst enrichment plants and thus playing their part in the weapons production cycle.

Risley

BNFL's head office at Risley in Cheshire houses the company's administration and inevitably deals with a proportion of defence-related work. According to Energy Under-Secretary Norman Lamont in 1981, Risley's activities 'are in support of the main activities of BNFL, which are largely directed towards the civil nuclear power programme'.[34] No indication has been given of the precise division of work, and words like 'largely' can be used to cover a multitude of sins. Lamont did add that 'some work related to contracts for the Ministry of Defence is carried out but this represents only a small fraction of the total activity on the site'.[35]

Harwell

The UKAEA, which until the early 1970s ran every aspect of military and civil atomic energy, is now primarily a research and development organisation centred, as in the past, on the Harwell establishment in Berkshire. Although the bulk of its work for several years has been concerned with civil nuclear research and to an increasing extent research into non-nuclear energy sources, it still carries out some ill-defined military work. According to Lamont again:

> Inevitably some of the facilities and expertise at Harwell in the nuclear field can have military application as well as civil and where it is in the public interest to do so some of the work has been directed to such ends. But such activities do not represent a major part of the total programme and are carried out under contract to the appropriate military establishment.[36]

Information has come to light about one of Harwell's part-military activities. Working with fissile material and on submarine reactors inevitably gives rise to quantities of medium-level radioactive waste. It seems that Harwell has the job of packaging such waste from Aldermaston, and handling that from the naval dockyards, before it is taken via the small port of Sharpness on the Severn to be dumped at sea.[37] In 1980 at an estimated overall fee of £12,000, Harwell managed the disposal in this way of 90 tonnes of radioactive waste from Chatham dockyard and 20 tonnes from Rosyth.[38] As Britain is one of the few countries which still persists in ocean-dumping, the practice has not surprisingly been the focus of mounting criticism.

Dounreay

The role that is and has been played by the UKAEA's Dounreay Fast Reactor Research Establishment in Caithness on the north coast of Scotland is intriguing. In 1960, the UKAEA revealed that they had been eagerly helping the Royal Navy by providing facilities and accommodation at Dounreay 'together with help in the establishment of the Admiralty's development and training programme'.[39] The end result, 20 years on, is HMS *Vulcan*, the navy's special reactor test station run by Rolls Royce and

Associates on a site adjacent to the Dounreay Prototype Fast Reactor.

Rolls Royce and Associates is a consortium employing about 1,400 staff (of whom 340 work at Dounreay) with a 43 per cent shareholding owned by Rolls, the rest being shared equally between Foster Wheeler, Vickers and Babcock and Wilcox. It was set up in 1959 by the Ministry of Defence to organise the purchase of a pressurised water reactor (PWR) manufactured by the US company Westinghouse for Britain's first nuclear-powered submarine, the HMS *Dreadnought*. In 1965 the company commissioned its first prototype reactor at HMS *Vulcan* for development and training, becoming the only private company in Britain to operate a power reactor. By 1980, Rolls had supplied the navy with 15 PWRs, and had at least another eight reactors in prospect.[40] In 1981 it was revealed that a second prototype reactor, designated PWR 2, was being built at HMS *Vulcan* mainly to provide a testing facility for the larger type of PWR that is due to power the Trident submarines,[41] the fourth generation of submarine reactor developed by the company. With over 17 years of working experience with PWRs, Rolls Royce is making a strong bid for a share in the construction of any commercial electricity-producing PWR in Britain.[42] The Central Electricity Generating Board, in promoting its plans to build a commercial PWR at Sizewell in Suffolk, does not draw attention to the fact that over the last two decades a similar, but much smaller, reactor has been powering Britain's nuclear submarine fleet, based on designs that have been tested and improved by Rolls Royce for the navy at the supposedly 'civil' site at Dounreay. Since 1960 the UKAEA's Safety and Reliability Directorate has been giving advice to the navy on the safety aspects of PWRs, a service they are still performing in relation to 'PWR 2' at HMS *Vulcan*.[43] The Dounreay establishment apparently also provides some unspecified 'minor services' to the Atomic Weapons Research Establishment at Aldermaston.[44]

In June 1981 the UKAEA began 'secret' shipments of plutonium nitrate by sea from Dounreay to Windscale, watched by the press and anti-nuclear activists. For the industry these journeys were a crucial step in proving the feasibility of the fast reactor fuel cycle: for the opposition they heralded what has become known as the 'plutonium economy'.

Plutonium, extracted from ordinary reactor spent fuel and made into mixed plutonium/uranium oxide fuel at Windscale, is transported to Dounreay to load into the 250 megawatt prototype fast reactor (PFR). After it has been 'burnt', the fuel plus its surrounding blanket of uranium is put through the small Dounreay reprocessing plant to separate plutonium for eventual re-use in the PFR. The UKAEA revealed that during 1981 they reprocessed 1.2 tonnes of uranium and plutonium fuel and extracted 200 kilogrammes of plutonium.[45] Because there is no plutonium fuel fabrication plant at Dounreay (and the UKAEA say it is too expensive to build one), extracted plutonium in a nitrate solution regularly has to be shipped back to the Windscale plant before it can be recycled in the PFR.

It takes between two and ten kilogrammes of plutonium to manufacture an atomic bomb.[46] According to Energy Under-Secretary Norman Lamont, each of the two containers used in each trip between Dounreay and Windscale has a design capacity of 'a few tens of kilogrammes' of plutonium.[47] Given that seven shipments are expected every year,[48] this gives a possible total annual cargo of more than 400 kilogrammes. In other words, enough plutonium for between 40 and 200 atomic bombs could be shipped around the Scottish coast every year.

Plutonium nitrate is the most sensitive material in the nuclear fuel cycle. Apart from being extremely toxic, it is in a form very close to pure plutonium metal. It has been convincingly shown that any kind of reactor-produced plutonium could be used in the fabrication of an atomic bomb.[49] The Royal Commission on Environmental Pollution concluded in 1976 that the 'construction of a crude nuclear weapon by an illicit group is credible'.[50] Thus the shipments have to be constantly guarded by an armed posse of the UKAEA's 'special constables' and subjected to other security measures in order to minimise the horrifying consequences of theft. As one nuclear power enthusiast, Professor J.M. Fremlin, put it: 'All we have to do is to use the same transport and escort system for plutonium shipments as we do for finished bombs'.[51]

The fuel for the fast reactor, envisaged by the industry as one of Britain's main suppliers of electricity in future decades, is effectively the same as the 'fuel' for atomic bombs. If the industry has its way, huge quantities of weapons-usable material will be regularly transported around the country and it will be impossible to guarantee the prevention of theft. Dounreay is carrying us over the threshold towards a society where the supply of civilian electricity will become dependent on the widespread circulation of a primarily military material.

A further problem concerns the technical impossibility of accurately accounting for nuclear materials in the fuel cycle. The industry expects each year to find some 'material unaccounted for' (MUF) but tells us reassuringly that any apparent loss 'does not necessarily mean that a real loss has been incurred'.[52] Over the decade up to 1980, a total of 111 kilogrammes of highly enriched uranium were 'lost' at Dounreay in seven years, while in three years there was an apparent 'gain' of nearly seven kilogrammes. At Windscale over the same period 119 kilogrammes of plutonium were 'lost' in four years, while 72 kilogrammes were 'found' in six. In 1979-80 11.2 kilogrammes of highly enriched uranium were 'lost' at Dounreay, while 5.5 kilogrammes of plutonium were 'found' at Windscale.[53] Whilst clearly such MUF figures do not *necessarily* mean that a loss or theft has occurred, the inevitable corollary is that a theft of enough fissile material to make several atomic bombs could occur without it ever being detected.

Aldermaston

The Atomic Weapons Research Establishment at Aldermaston in Berkshire is officially described as 'a self-contained centre for scientific and engineering development of advanced nuclear technology for both defence and civil purposes'.[54] It is well known as Britain's major nuclear weapons centre, providing the scientific and technical back-up necessary for the country's stockpile of warheads. It manufactures nuclear weapons components which are sent to the nearby Royal Ordnance Factory at Burghfield to be assembled into complete weapons. Responsibility for Aldermaston was transferred from the UKAEA to the Ministry of Defence in 1973. There are two research reactors on the site – 'Herald', Britain's most powerful light water research reactor which came into use in 1960, and 'Viper', a very high-powered 'fast-pulsed' reactor designed to produce short bursts of neutron and gamma radiation. At the end of 1980 the Ministry of Defence announced that they were building new plutonium processing facilities on the site, presumably in preparation for the introduction of the Trident missile system.[55] Aldermaston's military facilities also carry out a number of civil tasks. The site's most frequent customer 'for historical reasons' is the UKAEA, which has been given 'substantial support on civil projects, particularly in the development of the prototype fast reactor'.[56] During the 1960s and early 1970s Aldermaston carried out an 'extensive programme' related to fast reactor fuel fabrication.[57] The MoD's associated explosive testing facility on Foulness Island does work on the safety of reactor structures and has direct links with the European atomic energy agency, Euratom.

Uranium Mining and the Rössing connection

Without uranium there would be no nuclear power or nuclear weapons. Yet its mining is rarely mentioned in nuclear industry handouts because it does not happen on our doorsteps. Uranium comes from abroad, the main sources being Canada, America, Africa and Australia. Most of the uranium deposits have been found in the ancestral lands of American Indian, Eskimo and Aborigine populations, and it is these indigenous peoples who suffer most from the dirty and hazardous business of uranium extraction. Any kind of mining is environmentally damaging, but uranium mining creates a special hazard – radiation. The US Public Health Service has estimated that out of a total of 6,000 men who have worked underground in US uranium mines, between 600 and 1,100 will die of lung cancer caused by radiation exposure while working.[58] The incidence of leukaemia and cancer among white Australian uranium miners has been found to be six times the expected norm.[59]

Uranium for Britain's nuclear weapons programme originally came from four main sources: the Belgian Congo, the South African Rand goldfield and the Rum Jungle and Radium Hill mines in Australia. In 1970 it was revealed that the British government had signed a contract two years earlier with the British-based mining multinational Rio Tinto Zinc (RTZ) to supply 7,500 tons of uranium from their Rössing mine in Namibia – one of the largest opencast mines in the world. Namibia is illegally occupied by South Africa in defiance of a United Nations decree and a ruling by the International Court of Justice. Forty-five per cent of Britain's uranium now comes from

Namibia, having to be virtually smuggled here via France.[60]

RTZ has a powerful influence on British politics, having co-opted senior politicians onto its board: the Conservative Foreign Secretary Lord Carrington, for example, was a director of RTZ while the party was in opposition before 1979. The company have also established close links with the UKAEA: the former RTZ Chairman, Sir Val Duncan, has recalled the time he went to the UKAEA in search of contracts and left with a brief to 'find uranium and save civilisation'.[61]

The origins of the Rössing contract are instructive. Negotiations between RTZ and the Labour government took place in secret between 1965 and 1968. Ministry of Technology (MinTech) officials originally got together with representatives of the UKAEA and RTZ to secure the supply of 6,000 tons of uranium from a RTZ subsidiary in Canada, Rio Algom. In the small print of the briefing sent to the Cabinet, MinTech implied that the uranium might not be forthcoming from Canada, in which case it would come from an RTZ supplier in South Africa: no mention was made of Namibia as a potential source. The Foreign Secretary at the time asked that the Cabinet should be informed if the contract was to be switched.

In fact it seems that it had already been agreed with RTZ, without the knowledge of the Cabinet, that the uranium should come from Namibia. MinTech said as much to the Foreign Office in 1969, but the Cabinet was not immediately informed. The Cabinet was apparently manipulated by its advisers, the UKAEA and MinTech, to secure the outcome for RTZ. Tony Benn accused the UKAEA and RTZ of not being 'altogether candid', adding that what had happened pointed to 'the need for even greater vigilance than has been shown in the past. As the minister responsible at the time, I certainly learned that lesson'.[62]

Before their re-election in 1974, the Labour Party passed a resolution at their annual conference demanding the termination of the Rössing contract: less than a year later, Labour's Foreign Secretary announced that the contract would remain. At the same time he admitted that South Africa's occupation of Namibia was illegal, but said that South Africa had to be recognised as the 'de facto administering authority'. As the taxes and revenues paid by the Rössing operators went straight to South Africa, it was clear that hypocrisy had won the day.

The political storm aroused by the Rössing saga prompted the electricity boards in association with BNFL in 1979 to set up the British Civil Uranium Procurement Directorate, in an attempt to find uranium supplies of a less politically dubious origin and to break the RTZ/Whitehall stranglehold. The organisation's title implies that there are alternative arrangements for obtaining uranium for nuclear weapons, but in 1980 the Defence Minister, Francis Pym, claimed that 'no uranium ore is currently being purchased for military purposes'.[63] There is some, admittedly patchy, evidence which suggests that the Rössing contract is in fact supplying uranium for Britain's nuclear weapons programme.[64] Pym may however be technically correct in that for the time being existing stocks obviate the 'need' to buy uranium ore for weapons.

Low-level Radiation

Radiation is an inescapable result of the processing of uranium for weapons or power. The effects of exposing human beings to high levels of radiation were horrifyingly illustrated by the dropping of atom bombs on Hiroshima and Nagasaki. The effects of smaller doses of radiation have been a matter of great scientific controversy ever since, although the risks associated with so-called 'low-level' radiation have only recently become a focus of concern amongst workers in the nuclear industry and the public.

The international body which recommends limits on radiation exposure is the International Commission on Radiological Protection (ICRP), formed in London in 1928. ICRP has acquired a reputation as an independent scientific advisory body on radiation effects: in fact it is a self-perpetuating club, whose recommendations are increasingly coming under attack for seriously underestimating the risk of cancer and genetic damage caused by radiation exposure. In Britain the National Radiological Protection Board (NRPB) has the responsibility of assessing ICRP standards. Formed in 1970, it took over the research and advice-giving functions that had hitherto been performed by the Medical Research Council and the UKAEA, and was part of a general move to separate the promotional and regulatory functions which had been vested in the UKAEA. In 1976 the Royal Commission on Environmental Pollution strongly criticised the NRPB for its lack of independence and recommended its reconstitution at board level. The commission drew attention to the fact that the NRPB was based at Harwell and that it employed many former UKAEA staff.[65] A.S. McLean, the director up to his death in 1981, had been the UKAEA's Director of Health and Safety at Risley between 1957 and 1960. Revision of the NRPB board has taken place, although McLean's successor is John Dunster – another former UKAEA employee.

As more knowledge about the effects of radiation has been obtained, limits on exposure have been reduced: from 50 rems per year in 1925 to the current limits of 5 rems per year for workers in the nuclear industry and 0.5 rems per year for the public. It is crucial to realise that these do not represent 'safe' limits: it is now almost universally accepted that there is *no* safe level of exposure to radiation. Any amount is potentially damaging. The limits are set on the basis of what is considered to be an 'acceptable' risk. The cost of installing new technology to control the release of radiation is balanced against the cost of losing hours of work due to workers being exposed to that radiation. Most people do not realise that the nuclear industry plays this grim game of money for lives.

The effects of low-level radiation have been estimated mainly by extrapolation from the effects observed by the populations of Hiroshima and Nagasaki. The organisation responsible for collecting the data from the bomb-stricken cities is the American Atomic Bomb Casualty Commission (ABCC). Scientists from many countries have called for an international investigation into the methodology and findings of the ABCC, claiming that it is unreasonable to base a decision which may have vital implications for health on data screened and released by the US military.[66] Recent evidence from the US Lawrence Livermore Laboratory has questioned the basic results and conclusions of the ABCC research, and suggested that the ICRP has underestimated the risk from low-level radiation exposure by factors of between three and ten.[67] Several studies, mostly involving military workers, back up this theoretical analysis, finding higher rates of cancer than the ICRP would predict amongst exposed populations.[68]

A substantial body of evidence has also been accumulated about the effects of US nuclear weapons tests in the Nevada desert, which started in 1945 and still continue. Because it is not possible to *prove* the link between radiation from the tests and the cancer deaths of those in the area, no compensation has so far been paid out – although President Carter did order an inquiry into the radiation victims' claims, estimated to total at least a billion dollars.[69]

Evidence that nuclear submarine dockyards in Britain are dangerous to workers' health comes from a study of the workforce at Rosyth in Scotland. Two hundred workers were surveyed for ten years for possible chromosome damage and were found to have up to a four-fold increase in blood chromosome aberrations at exposures of less than five rems per year. Whether such damage is likely to lead to cancer is a matter of fierce debate, yet there are no plans to systematically follow up the workers.[70] Rosyth also provides an example of how health and safety standards are being put at risk by excessive secrecy. Dockyard workers there have been denied vital radiation exposure records which would enable them to judge the acceptability or otherwise of working conditions. Information on exposure levels is not published by the Ministry of Defence on any regular basis, although they will on request provide a blanket figure of unknown accuracy for all three nuclear submarine dockyards (Rosyth, Chatham and Devonport). Former dockyard workers comprise the only group of nuclear workers who are not going to be brought into the NRPB's massive register of radiation workers in Britain, which they began compiling in 1978. In spite of the dearth of information, there are some indications, mainly from employees at Rosyth, that exposure levels have been alarmingly high.[71]

Information available on BNFL's semi-military plants paints a similarly disturbing picture. Figures for 1975–78 published by the Health and Safety Executive suggest that less than one per cent of workers at the mainly 'civil' nuclear power stations run by the electricity boards were exposed to over 1.5 rems a year, while none went over the five rem limit. In striking contrast, comparable figures for Calder Hall, Chapelcross and Windscale show that over a fifth of workers – more than a thousand every year – were exposed to over 1.5 rems a year: there were even seven unfortunate souls at Windscale who received more than the five rem limit.[72] Between 1977 and 1981 a total of over £200,000 was paid out in compensation by BNFL to the widows of five Windscale workers who died of cancer or leukaemia that could well have been radiation-induced. The Treasury, on behalf of the Ministry of Defence, paid compensation to another widow whose husband had worked at Windscale. All the settlements were made out of court, enabling BNFL technically to avoid liability and to deny that radiation was the proven cause of death.[73]

Nuclear power and the American weapons connection

The key to understanding the precise relationship between nuclear power and weapons lies in an attempt to trace the source and destination over the years of Britain's weapons-grade fissile material – its highly-enriched uranium and plutonium. If we can map out the flows of these two potential nuclear explosives, we will be in a position to grasp the nature and extent of the civil/military connections. Inevitably, faced with the familiar problem of official secrecy,[74] we can advance only by combining detective work with informed estimates of probabilities.

A persistent problem with any analysis is the absence of any certain information on the proportion of weapons that incorporate plutonium as opposed to highly-enriched uranium. It seems likely, however, that Britain's early atomic fission bombs used plutonium. The later weapons programmes, based on the combination of fission and fusion reactions which produces a thermonuclear explosion (the H-bomb), at first used highly-enriched uranium in the 'trigger' fission bomb, and subsequently may have used a mixture of plutonium and highly-enriched uranium. Some H-bombs, perhaps including the smaller designs, may just use plutonium as the 'trigger' explosive.[75] The fusion reaction in Britain's H-bombs seems to depend on a regular supply of tritium.

There is little doubt, as described earlier, that during the late 1950s and early 1960s highly-enriched uranium from Capenhurst was fuelling Britain's growing stockpile of H-bombs, while plutonium from the original Windscale piles and then from the Calder Hall and Chapelcross reactors, was being used in the construction of atom bombs. Official references to the early roles of Calder Hall and Chapelcross openly mention their 'optimisation' for weapons purposes.[76] In 1963, however, the production

Nuclear sites in Britain

- HMS Vulcan
- Dounreay
- Rosyth
- Coulport
- Faslane
- Holy Loch
- Hunterston
- Torness
- Chapelcross
- Hartlepool
- Windscale
- Calder Hall
- Heysham
- Springfields
- Risley
- Menwith Hill
- Wylfa
- Capenhurst
- Trawsfynydd
- Molesworth
- Sizewell
- Berkeley
- Aldermaston
- Burghfield
- Bradwell
- Oldbury
- Harwell
- Chatham
- Hinkley Point
- Greenham Common
- Dungeness
- Devonport
- Winfrith

- ◆ US nuclear bases
- ⊙ Nuclear power stations, operating or under construction
- ● Other key sites in the fuel and weapons cycle
- ■ Research and administration
- ▲ Nuclear submarine bases

of bombs-grade uranium at Capenhurst appears to have halted and in 1964 the military demand for reactor-produced plutonium decreased. What has happened since 1964 has nowhere been satisfactorily explained. Has the Ministry of Defence relied upon large British supplies of weapons-grade fissile material, or obtained it from elsewhere, or both?

That a continued supply of weapons-grade material was necessary cannot be doubted. Four nuclear-powered Polaris submarines carrying a total of 192 nuclear warheads were deployed in the mid-to-late 1960s, and later 'modernised' under the £1,000 million Chevaline programme. By 1981 British-made bombs, assigned to NATO, could be carried by four squadrons of Jaguar and five squadrons of Buccaneer strike aircraft, as well as six squadrons of Vulcan bombers. In addition, a wide range of helicopters (Sea King, Wessex, Wasp and Lynx) are all capable of delivering nuclear depth charges. According to Defence Secretary John Nott: 'In all there are several hundred strike aircraft and helicopters capable of delivering United Kingdom nuclear weapons'.[77] One conservative unofficial estimate of Britain's stockpile adds in the battlefield warheads and ammunition and suggests a minimum total of 1,400 warheads in 1981.[78]

The solution to the mystery requires an examination of the amounts of plutonium created by Britain's nuclear power stations. The most comprehensive official analysis of UK plutonium production to date, provided to Robin Cook MP, says that up to the end of 1981, 33 tonnes had been created in all the Magnox reactors run by the electricity boards.[79] But according to our calculations using the government's own information on the plutonium production rates of Magnox stations, these reactors should have produced around 47.5 tonnes. So there appears to be some 14.5 tonnes of plutonium created by civil reactors, the location of which is unknown. These figures do not include the officially secret amounts of plutonium produced by the admittedly military reactors run by BNFL at Calder Hall and Chapelcross. Again we reckon that these two stations should have produced about 8.5 tonnes. So all in all, there seems to be more than 20 tonnes of plutonium in existence over and above that which is officially acknowledged (for our detailed calculations see Appendix 2).

We have little doubt that this unaccounted-for plutonium

has been put to military use – it is enough for perhaps 2-4,000 nuclear warheads. A proportion must have been used in Britain's warheads both before and after 1964, although it is doubtful whether British weapons stockpiles have been large enough to absorb anything like the whole amount. Thus there is still some plutonium the destination of which is unknown. Where has it gone?

For the answer it is necessary to turn to early British/US defence agreements covering the development of atomic energy. An '*Agreement . . . for cooperation on the uses of atomic energy for mutual defence purposes*', allowing the transfer of highly enriched uranium from the US to Britain for use as submarine fuel, was signed in 1958. The following year it was extended to cover nuclear weapons ingredients: the US sent their highly enriched uranium and tritium to Britain for use in warheads in exchange for British plutonium for US weapons, in the ratio of 1 gram of plutonium for each 1.76 grams of uranium 235. The swop was originally envisaged to involve 6.7 tonnes of plutonium and to last until 1969.[80]

The plutonium swop was renewed in 1969, 1970 and again in 1975. During the late 1970s, presumably because of President Carter's stand on nuclear non-proliferation, there was some doubt over whether the agreement would continue beyond the end of the decade. The Ministry of Defence thus made arrangements to ensure the maintenance of supply: the Chapelcross tritium plant was built and the Capenhurst plant for producing highly enriched uranium planned.

In 1981 the UKAEA said that the swop was only extended up to the end of 1979:[81] in fact the agreement was renewed in Washington by the Conservative government on 5 December 1979, coming into force on 25 March 1980 and due to last until the end of 1984.[82] The Ministry of Defence confirmed to us in 1981 that under the agreement, Britain is receiving highly enriched uranium for military purposes and that 'transactions take place from time to time'. It is presumed, given the completion of the Chapelcross tritium plant in 1980, that the transfer of tritium under the agreement no longer takes place.

The conclusion – that since 1959 Britain has been exporting its 'spare' plutonium to the United States – has frightening implications. Prime Minister Sir Alec Douglas-Home made it plain in 1964 that some of the plutonium extracted from Britain's Magnox reactors after Calder Hall and Chapelcross was destined to be sent to the US as part of the swop.[83] Plutonium manufactured by Britain's power stations has not only been used in British weapons (which is bad enough), but in American nuclear weapons: we are fuelling the US arms race.

More recently it has been revealed that Britain has agreed in principle to the further sale of several tonnes of plutonium to the US, allegedly for use in the US fast reactor programme.[84] Discussions on this deal have to be seen in the context of an emerging US shortage of all kinds of plutonium. With President Reagan giving the go-ahead to fast reactor development at Clinch River in Tennessee, and planning to add perhaps 14,000 new nuclear warheads to the US stockpile by 1990, future demands for plutonium are going to be heavy. The envisaged shortage has prompted the US Department of Energy to suggest that they could extract the plutonium contained in the 4,000 tonnes of spent fuel accumulated from US civil nuclear power stations and, using a newly-developed laser technique, purify it to weapons-grade. One critic has pointed out that this proposal if adopted would 'render the distinction between atoms for peace and atoms for war totally meaningless',[85] and the International Atomic Energy Agency has privately warned that it could 'unleash a new wave of European hostility towards nuclear energy'.[86] Purchasing the 'excess' plutonium created in Britain is an attractive option for the US. Although it could be arranged that plutonium bought from Britain was just used in fast reactor work, clearly its availability would enable the US to divert more of their home-produced plutonium into weapons production. It would be misleading to suggest that any British/US deal had nothing to do with the US weapons programme. As one worried scientist from the Central Electricity Generating Board has pointed out:

> If the United Kingdom sells plutonium from its Magnox programme to the United States there can be little doubt that this will lead to the vertical proliferation of nuclear weapons . . . [and] I do not think it could be rationally maintained that we, the United Kingdom, have distinguished civil use from military use.[87]

Although Britain appears to have a surplus of plutonium in the early 1980s, by the end of the century the situation could have changed. As well as providing plutonium to the US, the British nuclear industry is anxious to develop its own large-scale fast reactor which if built could use between six and ten tonnes of plutonium.[88] The expansion in the weapons programme proposed with Trident and by developing nuclear-capable Tornado strike attack aircraft, could also consume Magnox-created plutonium stocks. Assuming the completion of new reprocessing facilities at Windscale, some extra plutonium might become available from the advanced gas-cooled reactors and perhaps from a pressurised water reactor or two, although this would not be a huge amount as these reactors are relatively inefficient plutonium-producers.[89] The Magnox reactors – by far the most efficient plutonium-producers – will begin to reach the end of their useful lives by 1990 and could all be out of service by the year 2000. If at that stage the British government was anxious to maintain or augment its nuclear weapons, it would probably have to find new sources of plutonium or highly-enriched uranium. We may find, in other words, that today's plutonium surplus will become tomorrow's shortage.

Overt military pressure on the civil industry has increased substantially over recent years with the Ministry of Defence decisions to start production of tritium and highly-enriched uranium. This could be a pattern that is repeated in the future as the Ministry of Defence, faced with a shortage of weapons material, demand new plutonium production reactors or enrichment plants.

3.

Atoms for Peace?

> The nuclear power industry is unintentionally contributing to an increased risk of nuclear war. *The Fox Report, 1976, on uranium mining in Australia*

At 4 p.m. on 7 June 1981, fourteen Israeli planes took off from Etzion air base in Sinai and headed east. Flying in tight formation, the planes were mistaken for one commercial aircraft by Jordanian radar operators. An hour and a half later, the planes had reached their target: Iraq's nuclear reactor 'Osirak' outside Baghdad. Eight F16s made a series of passes over Osirak and dropped their payload of 16 tons of TNT. Within two minutes they had disappeared, leaving behind a badly damaged reactor building, a few puffs of anti-aircraft flak and a fearsome new twist in the dangerous game of nuclear proliferation.

The Israeli Prime Minister's announcement of the raid stunned the international community. The official statement claimed that Israel had been observing the construction of the Osirak reactor with growing concern. It quoted 'sources whose reliability is beyond doubt' as confirming that Iraq was using Osirak to make nuclear weapons for use against Israel, despite Iraq having signed the Nuclear Non-Proliferation Treaty (NPT). Allegations were made that Iraq had purchased nuclear technology which could only have been useful for military purposes, and that a 'secret chamber' had been constructed underground where Iraqi scientists were to develop their bomb. The Israelis had acted at that time, they said, because the first shipment of highly enriched uranium fuel for the reactor was about to be delivered.

The bombing of Osirak is merely the latest illustration of two key non-proliferation issues: the role of 'civil' nuclear technology in fostering the spread of nuclear weapons, and the total inability of governments, international agencies and treaties to control that spread. After the bombing, Israel was universally condemned, but the opinion remained that it was right in one respect: Iraq's nuclear intentions were military, not civil.

Iraq's experience in nuclear technology extends as far back as 1959, when a Soviet research centre was built at Tuwaitha near Baghdad. Then, as now, Iraq had no public plans for developing a nuclear power programme. In 1968, Iraq began negotiations with France for the sale of a large reactor, the chief negotiator then being Saddam Hussein, Iraq's President when Osirak was bombed. Hussein called this contract 'the first Arab attempt designed to obtain nuclear armaments'. France would not sell a large reactor (of the type France itself had used to make nuclear weapons), but eventually, in 1975, a contract was signed for delivery of two smaller 'research reactors', and the 84 kilogrammes of highly enriched uranium required to fuel them.[1]

News of the contract leaked out, to be greeted by vociferous protest. France could not withdraw from the deal – too much money was involved, and Iraq was, and is, a major oil supplier – but they did offer a substitute fuel which was not potential bomb material, being enriched to only 7 per cent. The Iraqis however refused this so-called 'Caramel' fuel on the, perhaps, reasonable grounds that it was new and relatively unproven. France compromised by agreeing to ship the highly enriched fuel in lots smaller than could be used for weapons.

Iraq proceeded, however, to add to its nuclear activities. By irradiating natural uranium in a reactor, non-fissile uranium 238 atoms are transmuted into plutonium 239. If the fuel is removed after only a short time in the reactor, there is a high concentration of plutonium 239 which can be separated out and used as bomb material. A large supply of natural uranium and a chemical separation plant are therefore required for this end.

Iraq has gone to great lengths to secure supplies of uranium ore, signing contracts with Portugal, Libya and Brazil, despite such uranium being unsuitable as fuel for its reactors. Iraq has also bought 'hot cell' equipment from Italy, which would handle radioactive fuel from the reactor and help extract the plutonium from that fuel by shielding operators from the radioactivity. Since the French contract specifies that spent fuel will be returned to France for reprocessing, there is no need for Iraq to buy such technology except for covert military operations.[2]

Israel's intelligence experts began to worry about Iraq's nuclear intentions in 1976, when its nuclear budget jumped from $5m to $70m per year, and Iraqi delegations went shopping for nuclear hardware. Israel's counter-measures were at first low-key, urging greater caution among Western countries dealing with Iraq. Nothing happened, it being pointed out that Iraq had signed the NPT and its facilities were subject to safeguards and inspections by the International Atomic Energy Agency (IAEA). When diplomacy failed, Israel's secret service, Mossad, began covert operations against Iraq's nuclear programme. In April 1979, unknown saboteurs – Mossad agents according to some – attempted to blow up the core of the Osirak reactor at Toulon in France while it was awaiting shipment to Iraq, holding up delivery for a year. In 1980, Yahia Meshad, the Egyptian-born head of Iraq's nuclear programme, was found bludgeoned to death in a Paris hotel room. Several weeks later, a French prostitute said to have been a key witness to Meshad's death was killed by a hit-and-run driver. Later that year, bombs wrecked the Rome offices of SNIA Technit, the Italian company that had sold Iraq the hot cell technology. In September 1980, in the first week of the Iran-Iraq war, Osirak was slightly damaged in an air attack by Phantom jets. The Phantoms bore the markings of the Iranian air force, but were generally thought to have been Israeli planes getting a close look at Osirak. Following the air raid, Hussein declared that Iran had nothing to fear from Iraq's nuclear capability, as any weapons would be used against the 'Zionist enemy'.

The Iraqis at first refused permission to the IAEA to inspect the damage done to the reactor, which at that time had just received a shipment of 12 kilogrammes of enriched uranium fuel, by claiming that 'the NPT did not hold in times of war'.[3] The reactor was only inspected again in January 1981, four months later. Such an idiosyncratic interpretation of the NPT only served to heighten suspicions that Iraq's intentions were military and to damage the IAEA's credibility, as they could not gain access to the reactor despite repeated requests.

The Iraqi response to the 1981 raid was in itself revealing. The Revolutionary Command Council issued a statement saying Israel knew that 'a liberated and powerful Iraq would sooner or later represent a decisive element in determining the outcome of the struggle against it . . . the enemies will not be able to weaken our power to make progress, whether in the technological, scientific, social or economic fields'.[4]

It cannot be proved that Iraq was making a bomb, but it is likewise impossible to categorically deny it. The possibility of Iraq following the plutonium route to nuclear weapons has been confirmed by the former head of the French Commissariat à l'Energie, Francis Perrin.[5] The important point here is that Iraq played it by the rules: it signed the NPT and agreed to IAEA safeguards, the two main methods of attempting to ensure that 'civil' nuclear technology is not used to make nuclear weapons. Yet Iraq, along with many other countries which have signed the treaty and agreed to safeguards, is still in a position to make nuclear weapons.

To examine the fundamental – and unsolvable – problems in controlling the use of nuclear power to make nuclear weapons, it is necessary to return to the beginnings of the nuclear arms race.

Debate about how to control the awesome destructive potential of atomic energy was joined at the end of the second world war among United Nations countries. In 1946, a committee of distinguished US nuclear scientists and politicians produced a report on possibilities for the international control of atomic energy, the Lilienthal-Acheson Report, which was later modified as the US proposal to the UN on atomic energy control. The report proposed an international development agency which would carry out the 'dangerous' nuclear activities and would own all the uranium mines and plants producing fissile material. The 'safe' activities would be carried out in individual countries under the supervision of this agency.[6]

Nationalism and mutual mistrust defeated the objectives of setting up such an agency, the Soviet Union claiming that such an important industrial enterprise as atomic energy could not be intrusted to an anonymous supranational body which would have overriding sovereignty in atomic matters.

'Atoms for Peace'

Fundamental in creating the problem of nuclear weapons proliferation was the 'Atoms for Peace' programme announced by the US President Eisenhower in 1953, and its associated

Table 1: Proliferation risk research reactors

Research reactors in non-nuclear weapons states producing weapons-grade plutonium:

	Plutonium production 1980 *(kgs)*
Belgium (2 reactors)	35
Canada (3 reactors)	1851
West Germany	90
India	240
Israel	128
Italy	39
Japan	54
Norway	63
Switzerland	180
Taiwan	84
Yugoslavia	21

Research reactors in non-nuclear weapons states with weapons-grade uranium fuel:

Argentina	Israel	South Africa
Australia	Italy	Spain
Austria	Japan	Sweden
Belgium	Netherlands	Thailand
Canada	Pakistan	Turkey
Colombia	Poland	West Germany
Denmark	Romania	

Amounts of uranium required for one fuel load vary from over 20kgs in Spain, Poland and Italy, to more than 7kgs in West Germany. Combined fuel charges for all reactors in the country are above 7kgs in Belgium, Canada, Denmark, West Germany, Italy, Japan, Netherlands, Poland and Sweden. The total number of proliferation risk reactors is 59 in 25 countries. These figures do not include research reactors which, like the Osirak reactor, could be illicitly operated to produce weapons plutonium.

Based on Albert Wohlstetter *et al*, *Swords from Ploughshares*, University of Chicago Press 1979, pp. 168–69.

'Operation Candour', which released an avalanche of declassified US nuclear information. With the possibility of generating electricity from atomic energy clearly established, politicians and scientists were anxious to develop the potential, but in order to gain public support for this, the image of Hiroshima and Nagasaki had to be erased: the atom had to become 'peaceful'. Here is the source of the 'smokescreen' covering the relationship between nuclear power and nuclear weapons.

The Atoms for Peace programme offered knowledge, technical skill and financial subsidies to countries interested in atomic energy: some 26 research reactors were 'given away' with the hope, no doubt, of creating a market for US companies if these countries decided on a nuclear power programme.[7] Atoms for Peace was also conceived in the context of the Cold War, and Soviet atomic tests (A-bomb in 1949, H-bomb in 1953), and was therefore primarily seen as an instrument of foreign policy designed to capture influence and prestige for a 'generous' and 'peace-loving' United States. In December 1953, Eisenhower announced the plan to the United Nations in semi-religious terms:

> The United States pledges before you, and therefore before the whole world, its determination to help solve the fearful atomic dilemma – to devote its entire heart and mind to finding the way by which the miraculous inventiveness of man shall not be dedicated to his death, but consecrated to his life.[8]

Atoms for Peace, and the earlier UN debates on nuclear arms, upheld a policy of limiting nuclear weapons while encouraging the spread of nuclear power. The fear that nations might misuse a nuclear industry for the production of weapons was expressed at the time, but rejected by the majority of politicians and advisors. Their belief in a purely civil nuclear power industry was based on several scientifically flawed assumptions, which have proved to be of fearful importance in today's proliferation debate.

Firstly, it was thought that plutonium produced in civil reactors would be unsuitable for use in nuclear weapons. As civil nuclear fuel stays in a reactor longer, the proportion of the isotope plutonium 240 increases. Any explosive containing a high proportion of this isotope is relatively unstable, as Pu 240 fissions spontaneously and can therefore prematurely set off a chain reaction. It is still claimed by today's nuclear industry that civil reactor fuel cannot make a useful weapon, but research has now shown this to be incorrect.[9] More sophisticated bomb design is required, but this may be a small price to pay for having plutonium available in large quantities. The US has in fact tested a nuclear weapon with so-called 'reactor-grade' plutonium as the fissile material,[10] and it is now agreed, but not generally appreciated, that plutonium of any isotopic composition can be used in a nuclear weapon.[11] Thus civil spent nuclear fuel is potential bomb material if the plutonium can be chemically separated.

Secondly, it was assumed in the 1940s and 1950s that the manufacture of nuclear explosives for the military could only be achieved by 'complicated, difficult and expensive measures that could not remain undetected'.[12] This was an understandable assumption at the time, given the enormous size of the Manhattan Project, although the US was truly shocked when the Soviet Union tested its first bomb in 1949 well ahead of predicted schedules. But technology has inexorably advanced, until the requirements for making nuclear weapons materials are no longer so punitive, being in the range of tens of trained scientists and tens of millions of dollars.[13]

Finally, there was an overriding faith that inspection and control would be sufficient to detect any non-weapons state developing bombs from its nuclear power technology, although there was disagreement as to what sanctions could effectively be brought to bear on such states.

By the time these problems, unrecognised or even covered up by Atoms for Peace advocates, could be fully appreciated, there was little, in a technological sense, that could be done. By 1965, 42 non-weapons countries had research reactors, and were therefore building up knowledge and expertise in the nuclear field. By 1980, 21 non-weapons countries had operating nuclear power stations and associated plutonium in spent fuel; 10 had reprocessing facilities and one had an enrichment plant. By 1985, it was estimated, if plans made in 1975 were adhered to, nearly 40 non-weapons countries would have enough chemically separable plutonium in spent fuel produced by their nuclear reactors for a few bombs.[14] The nuclear genie was well and truly out of the bottle.

In 1946, the Lilienthal-Acheson plan had proposed a technological monopoly to prevent this genie escaping, recognising that international treaties and policing would prove to be weaker than the rivalries of nation states and the imperfections of human institutions:

> We have concluded that an attempt to give body to such a system of agreements through international cooperation holds no promise of adequate security.[15]

Yet international treaties and policing – the system which the Lilienthal-Acheson plan saw would be unenforceable – have been the very basis of proliferation controls in the past twenty years: the International Atomic Energy Agency (IAEA) set up in 1957, and the Non-Proliferation Treaty (NPT), signed in 1968.

The IAEA and nuclear proliferation safeguards

The IAEA system is basically unenforceable because it does not own 'dangerous' nuclear activities, it merely inspects, and because both 'dangerous' and 'safe' activities are governed by sovereign states. The IAEA is also bound by a paradox: it is a watchdog overseeing the production of fissile material for diversion to weapons, yet its main priority is to promote the growth of nuclear power. The largest proportion of the IAEA's budget is spent on information and technical assistance in support of nuclear power programmes.[16]

IAEA safeguards have in general been shaped by the nature of specific problems and by the degree to which countries will permit their nuclear industries to be regulated. The first safeguard system appeared in 1961, and applied to very small amounts of fissile material made in reactors under 100 megawatts; in 1965 this was extended to larger reactors. In 1966, reprocessing plants were included in the agreements and material in conversion and fuel fabrication plants was added in 1968. By this time, both China and France had tested nuclear weapons.

The IAEA system has two basic components: accounting methods designed to spot the loss of nuclear material, and regular inspection of seals placed on agreed facilities. Inspections have recently been augmented by video monitoring of the seals in some facilities.[17]

It is impossible to predict accurately, just how much fissile material has been produced inside a reactor, and how much will be 'lost in the system'. IAEA accountants can therefore never be sure if their assessment of 'Material Unaccounted For' (MUF) represents this unavoidable loss and uncertainty or whether it represents a diversion for military ends. This problem will be accentuated with the larger flow of fissile materials resulting from any growth in nuclear power. The IAEA allows for losses of up to 8kgs of plutonium, the amount it reckons 'significant' in making nuclear weapons, but in fact the limit is acknowledged to be nearer 4kgs,[18] which for larger nuclear programmes will be within the margins of error of the system.

The system can apparently tolerate large losses without the alarm being raised. In 1968, the IAEA's equivalent watchdog in Europe, Euratom, failed to prevent the illicit export of 200 tons of uranium oxide, even though they had to grant an export licence for its shipment. When it was discovered that the uranium had been diverted, most probably for Israel's nuclear weapons programme, Euratom covered up the affair until 1977.[19]

IAEA inspections have also come under fire for being inadequate. As of 1980, the IAEA Safeguards Department had 213 staff, 138 of whom were inspectors who have to cover 774 facilities.[20] Thus each facility is inspected only once or twice a year – a gap that could leave ample time for diversion by a determined party. Countries are warned of approaching inspection, and have in the past avoided inspection by claiming an area is out of bounds due to radioactive contamination. The total amount of fissile material under safeguards is relatively small: 5 tonnes of weapons-grade plutonium, 78 tonnes of plutonium in spent fuel and 11 tonnes of highly enriched uranium.[21]

The main problem with IAEA safeguards is that they are reactive, and not active, and no strong sanctions can be brought to bear on individual countries. In any case, safeguards can be circumvented by any determined state. As one commentator remarked, 'the safeguard procedures are more like a burglar alarm than locks on the door: it will tell you if a bank is being robbed, but it won't stop the break-in'.[22]

Only 11 days after the Israeli raid on Osirak, complacency

about IAEA safeguards was again shattered. Dr. Roger Richter, an IAEA inspector covering the Middle East and south-east Asia, resigned from the IAEA. He immediately flew to Washington and gave evidence to Congressional committees that 'the agency's safeguards were not adequate to detect violations of the NPT by Iraq'.[23] Dr Richter had written to the US State Department in 1980 alleging that 'the IAEA safeguards are totally incapable of detecting the production of plutonium in large-scale materials-test reactors' such as Osirak. Opinion on the committees was divided about the strength of Dr Richter's testimony, but the chairman of the Senate Foreign Relations Committee declared himself 'shaken'.

The IAEA's chairman at the time, Sigvard Eklund, reacted angrily to Richter's defection. Information gathered by IAEA inspection teams is deemed highly confidential, as IAEA rules are designed to protect each country's commercial and industrial secrets. (In the light of this requirement, it is interesting to note that the IAEA has never announced a single example of diversion of nuclear material.) So it was a severe blow to the system that an inspector should tell all on the day of his resignation. Dr Eklund expressed fears that Richter's behaviour would have repercussions for the ability of IAEA inspectors to gain acceptance and admittance at nuclear facilities, which would 'further complicate the process of designation of inspectors',[24] thereby highlighting the IAEA's weakness. As Dr Richter also had family connections with Israel, and his 'patch' covered that country, one cannot rule out political motives in Richter's defection, which raises a general question of who inspects the inspectors?

Internal dissension and argument are not unknown within the IAEA. In 1977, a leaked confidential document called for improvement in the control of nuclear materials in respect of a wide variety of facilities, and stated that it would be perfectly possible to cover up the diversion of fissile material by temporarily returning it to the installation about to be inspected. It confirms that countries can keep inadequate records of their fissile materials, thereby making satisfactory inspection impossible, yet incur no penalties.[25]

Thus there are grounds for supposing that safeguards on civil nuclear facilities to prevent diversion of fissile material to weapons are highly unsatisfactory, but that merely increasing

Table 2: Main points of the Non-Proliferation Treaty

Article I pledges nuclear weapons states not to transfer to non-nuclear weapons states or 'to any recipient whatsoever' nuclear weapons, or control over nuclear weapons, either directly or indirectly.

Article II pledges non-nuclear weapons states not to receive 'from any transfer whatsoever' nuclear weapons or control over them.

Article III requires non-nuclear weapons states to submit their nuclear facilities to IAEA safeguards to verify their compliance with the treaty; no party to the treaty may supply fissile material or the facilities to make such material, unless the recipient agrees to IAEA safeguards. Safeguards 'shall be implemented in a manner designed to comply with Article IV'.

Article IV reaffirms the 'inalienable' right to develop the peaceful uses of nuclear technology, and pledges parties to facilitate trade with this in mind.

Article V provides for sharing benefits of 'peaceful' nuclear explosions.

Article VI pledges parties to pursue negotiations in good faith to end the arms race and effect complete disarmament.

Article VII affirms the right of states to conclude regional non-proliferation treaties.

Article VIII provides for a review of the treaty at five-yearly intervals.

Article IX describes the process of ratification (agreeing to safeguards).

Article X provides that any party can withdraw from the treaty with three months' notice if the country decides that its supreme interests are in jeopardy.

employees and money within the IAEA will have little effect: the problems derive from political ineffectiveness and commitment to the wrong aim – mainly that of encouraging the growth of nuclear power.

The Non-Proliferation Treaty

The NPT entered into force in March 1970: by February 1981, 110 non-weapons states were party to the treaty, 78 of which had negotiated safeguards agreements with the IAEA. France, China, India, South Africa, Pakistan, India, Spain, Argentina and Brazil are all countries with significant nuclear activities which have not signed the NPT, although the last two have signed a regional non-proliferation treaty for South America and France has agreed to act as if it had signed the NPT.

The NPT embodies the same fundamental contradiction as the Atoms for Peace programme and IAEA statutes: a determination to halt the increase in nuclear weapons states while promoting the development of a 'peaceful' nuclear capacity which can in fact be converted into a military capability.

The articles of the NPT are set out in Table 2. The conditions imposed on non-weapons states by the letter of the NPT will not stop a determined government from diverting civil fissile material to military use. Components for nuclear weapons can be developed and stockpiled without infringing the treaty in any way. Any signatory can withdraw with 90 days' notice, if it judges that events related to the treaty 'have jeopardised the supreme interests of its country'. No nation has yet chosen to withdraw, but after the Israeli raid on Osirak, the IAEA was quoted as being worried that Iraq might withdraw, saying that the treaty afforded no protection from non-signatories.[26]

The NPT has failed in its prime objective of freezing the number of nuclear weapons states: since 1968, India, Israel and South Africa have developed nuclear capabilities, and a further half dozen or so countries are 'near-nuclear' (i.e. reckoned to be within 3-4 years of being able to test a nuclear weapon), resulting from equipment and materials supplied for supposedly 'peaceful' nuclear power programmes.

The NPT rests on a bargain between the nuclear weapons states and non-weapons states. The non-weapons states are free to develop nuclear power but have to forgo nuclear weapons, while the weapons states have undertaken to disarm. Article VI pledges nuclear weapons states to:

> pursue negotiations in good faith on effective measures relating to the cessation of the nuclear arms race at an early date, and to nuclear disarmament, and on a treaty of general and complete disarmament under strict and effective control.

Table 3: Power reactors in non-nuclear weapons states

NS=non-signatory;
R=ratified (i.e. IAEA safeguards in operation);
S=signed but not ratified

	NPT status	Amounts of separable plutonium by 1980 (kgs)
Argentina	NS	335
Austria	R	163
Belgium	R	1131
Brazil	NS	127
Bulgaria	R	618
Canada	R	4706
Czechoslovakia	R	324
Egypt	S	146 (1990)
Finland	R	339
East Germany	R	1172
West Germany	R	6667
Hungary	R	686 (1985)
India	NS	994
Italy	R	1500
Japan	R	7435
Korea	R	185
Luxembourg	R	98 (1985)
Mexico	R	829 (1985)
Netherlands	R	521
Pakistan	NS	167
Philippines	R	244 (1985)
Poland	R	309 (1990)
Romania	R	309 (1985)
South Africa	NS	576 (1985)
Spain	NS	1195
Sweden	R	3106
Switzerland	R	1527
Taiwan	R	355
Yugoslavia	R	96

Based on estimates in *Nuclear News*, August 1977, quoted in Albert Wohlstetter *et al*, *Swords from Ploughshares*, University of Chicago Press 1979, p. 183. Schedules may have slipped in some countries, and *Nuclear News* assumes a 65 per cent load factor, which may be too high, thus the figures should be taken as orders of magnitude only. NPT status is from *IAEA Bulletin*, vol. 23, no. 1, February 1981, p. 32.

But international diplomacy and negotiation have failed to prevent 'vertical' proliferation (the arms race), whilst the spread of weapons capability ('horizontal' proliferation) has continued.

A major complaint of non-weapons states at the 1975 and 1980 NPT review conferences was the failure of weapons states party to the treaty (Britain, the US and USSR) to live up to their side of the bargain and negotiate for disarmament. There is still no SALT II treaty, nor a comprehensive ban on nuclear weapons testing, which would be required to show 'good faith' on the part of the superpowers. Instead, the arms race is now accelerating: world military spending is now running at $500 thousand million in current (1980) prices, almost double what it was in 1960.[27] The Reagan Administration is determined to site cruise and Pershing II missiles in Europe, install the MX missile system, and deploy the neutron bomb, while the Soviet Union is deploying the SS20 missile and Britain decides to 'modernise' Polaris and purchase Trident. Vertical proliferation is essentially out of control.[28]

It is hardly surprising that non-weapons countries have seen through the hypocrisy of proliferation controls. The superpowers have not kept their side of the bargain and disarmed, so why should non-weapons states deny themselves the possibility of making their own nuclear weapons? India has refused to sign the NPT, viewing it as a tool wielded by the weapons states to keep the 'balance of terror' in their favour. The weapons states cannot expect others to remain without nuclear weapons when they demonstrate, by continually improving the size and quality of their nuclear arsenals, their belief that nuclear weapons have a high military and political value. The logical implication is the argument that nuclear disarmament could in fact be speeded up by non-weapons states acquiring nuclear capabilities – one that has already been made by black politicians:

> Only when the West and the Soviet block discover that they cannot make the rest of the world refrain from the nuclear dream unless they themselves give up the weapons, will the world at last address itself to the fundamentals of human survival.[29]

Non-weapons states do not even have the guarantee under the NPT that they will not be attacked with nuclear weapons. The superpowers have made declarations to the UN on the first use of nuclear weapons, but assurances are conditional and limited in scope.[30] Thus, in the face of the superpowers' reluctance to disarm, acquisition of nuclear weapons seems to become a vital 'deterrent' against the threat of annihilation.

The proliferation debate at best smacks of double standards, and at worst, racism. There is an implicit assumption that the existing weapons states are somehow more 'responsible' and can therefore be trusted with nuclear weapons, while non-weapons states cannot, thus disguising the fact that the non-weapons states are merely mimicking the strategy of deterrence employed by the superpowers. Because 'horizontal' proliferation will only be controlled if 'vertical' proliferation is controlled, weapons states have an obligation to disarm at the same time as enforcing proliferation controls, thereby reducing the motivation to acquire a nuclear 'deterrent' and reducing the tension in areas destabilised by the introduction of nuclear technology.

Other proliferation controls

In May 1974, the pretence that civil nuclear energy had nothing to do with nuclear weapons was irrevocably shattered by the explosion of a nuclear device by India. India had built up a very large scientific affort in the nuclear field, possessing research and power reactors, fuel fabrication facilities and a chemical separation plant, all of which was claimed to be for 'peaceful' purposes. Plutonium from India's Canadian-built reactor was reprocessed and used to make an explosive yielding 15 kilotons, slightly larger than the bomb dropped on Hiroshima. The explosion was a 'peaceful' one, India claimed, aimed at investigating the usefulness of nuclear explosions for civil engineering and the like.

In the wake of the test, an informal meeting took place between nuclear supplier countries to discuss more stringent proliferation controls on exports of nuclear technology and materials. This so-called 'London Club' (or Nuclear Suppliers Group) drew up a 'trigger list': an inventory of nuclear technology considered to be a proliferation risk. Items on the list were not to be sold unless the recipient country agreed to IAEA inspection. These rules are lacking in two respects: they do not insist on safeguards on *all* nuclear facilities, and they do not definitively exclude the export of 'sensitive' technology, being a set of

Table 4: Reprocessing and enrichment plants in non-nuclear weapons states (planned or operating)

	Reprocessing plants capable of making 3–6 nuclear weapons	Reprocessing plants capable of making 30–60 nuclear weapons	Enrichment plants
Brazil	●		●
South Korea	●		
Pakistan	●		●
Taiwan	●		
Argentina	●		●
Italy	●		
Japan	●		●
South Africa		●	●
Belgium		●	
Israel		●	●
West Germany		●	●
India		●	
Netherlands			●

Based on Albert Wohlstetter et al, *Swords from Ploughshares*, University of Chicago Press 1979, p. 16.

guidelines without any legal obligation. They also represent an attempt to present a solid front of industrialised countries against those who are building up a commercial nuclear industry outside the NPT and IAEA: Israel, Brazil and South Africa are, or will be, in a position to export nuclear technology outwith current proliferation restrictions.

In the spring of 1977, the Ford Foundation published an influential report on which President Carter based the Non-Proliferation Act, passed in 1978.[31] There was to be an embargo on the export of reprocessing and enrichment plants, tougher safeguards on all material and equipment supplied by the US and a ban on the reprocessing or transfer of spent fuel of US origin without US consent. Carter also called for an evaluation of the international fuel cycle, which duly took place (and of which more later).

President Reagan seems intent on dismantling these restrictions on nuclear exports, although the Israeli raid on Osirak seems to have modified his stance somewhat – India's contract with the US for enriched uranium for its Tarapur reactor is to be ended. Reagan has said that he believes the real strength of US proliferation policy lies with its reliability as a supplier. US credibility has been undermined by the recent proposal to reprocess the spent fuel from US nuclear power stations to yield plutonium for its expanding nuclear weapons programme:[32] the US is doing exactly what its proliferation policy tries to stop other countries doing.

South Africa

South Africa is a prime example of how the 'Atoms for Peace' programme has aided the spread of nuclear weapons. After 1945, when uranium was scarce, Britain and the US began large programmes to identify deposits and secure their output. Uranium had been discovered in South African goldfields, and huge amounts of money were poured into the area by the Combined Development Agency(CDA), the joint British and US war-time uranium procurer. From 1950 to 1967, uranium oxide was shipped to the US and Britain for their weapons programmes. The ancillary plant built by the CDA formed the basis of South Africa's own commercial uranium mining business. A nuclear research centre was established and work went ahead with the SAFARI-1 research reactor, supplied by the US under Atoms for Peace with fuel fabricated by Britain. Many South African scientists were trained in the US, and as the *Washington Post* commented, 'expert sources in the US are said to feel that the operation of SAFARI-1 was an essential element in the training of South African scientists who later developed the unsafeguarded enrichment process'.[33]

South African developed its enrichment technology with aid from West Germany, which has been collaborating for years with South Africa in military matters. A pilot enrichment plant at Valindaba started production in 1975, with plans to expand the plant and make South Africa into an international enriched uranium exporter. Ambiguous statements have been issued by the regime since its entry into the nuclear arena; claiming that its intentions were 'peaceful' while not renouncing the possibility that it might wish to make nuclear weapons. Ambiguity such as this is commonly used by nations aspiring to nuclear weapons:

> It may be simpler then to go most of the way under a civilian flag, trying to leave the world in uncertainty with shorter warning time, and with reduced possibilities for designing and enacting sanctions . . . civilian utilisation of nuclear energy may enable a state to make nuclear bombs without ever disclosing it.[34]

In July 1977, South African preparations for a nuclear test were detected in the Kalahari Desert.[35] This led to increased pressure to halt all nuclear collaboration with the apartheid regime. The western governments involved replied by repeating earlier claims that collaboration was essentially commercial, and argued that cooperation in the nuclear field should continue in order to persuade South Africa to sign the NPT. This twisted logic has not succeeded: collaboration has continued – France is building two nuclear power stations which would give South Africa plutonium for bombs – and South Africa has not signed the NPT.

In September 1979, a US satellite detected a low-yield nuclear explosion in the South Atlantic off the coast of South Africa. Despite international attempts to find other explanations for the atmospheric events detected by the satellite, the evidence suggests the testing of a small nuclear device (below 4 kilotons). It is estimated that the Valindaba enrichment plant could have produced a dozen such nuclear weapons.[36]

Without the aid of US, French, West German and British civil nuclear technology and expertise, South Africa would not be the nuclear power it is now reckoned to be. These countries have contravened the NPT by continuing to collaborate with South Africa on nuclear power while knowing of its military intentions. No other demonstration is needed of the ineffectiveness of diplomatic methods of proliferation control, nor of the duplicity of the nuclear industry's oft-repeated claim that 'No country has developed nuclear weapons from a civil nuclear power programme'.[37]

South Africa is just one example of a process that has been repeated in various ways in other countries which took up the Atoms for Peace offer. Thousands of nuclear scientists have been trained in western countries and returned to set up research centres in their own. Nuclear 'know how' must be obtained by any country wishing to develop nuclear power, but unavoidably, this knowledge can be used for military ends. All non-weapons countries with nuclear power are drifting towards higher and higher levels of competence in the nuclear field which, even if there is no definite aim to make nuclear weapons, will enable such weapons to be made if the political situation in these countries changes. Extending the NPT or increasing the efficiency of IAEA safeguards cannot control this situation: proliferation cannot be halted unless the nuclear industry is closed down.

Nuclear exporting

Yet the motivation to keep selling the technology and training the scientists is powerful. The history of the past 25 years, 'despite international safeguards, the Non-Proliferation Treaty, and various international cooperative arrangements suggests that in reality commercial considerations have tended to dominate security concerns, complicating and even undermining, efforts at control'.[38]

The money invested in nuclear power is enormous: the Manhattan Project cost the US taxpayer $2 billion (1945 prices), the British AGR programme is calculated to have cost £11 billion in 1981 prices.[39] Faced with dwindling orders for nuclear power stations, both world wide and domestically, corporations have to recoup substantial losses on their investments. General Atomic in the US lost $500 million on reactor sales and have left the business altogether while AEG Telefunken – a major partner in the German construction company Kraftwerk Union – has withdrawn, citing 1974 losses of $274-87 million on reactor sales.[40] Two nuclear power stations have recently been put into mothballs in the US because of soaring costs.[41]

There is fierce competition between the major nuclear suppliers for potentially lucrative export markets in the developing countries. US companies have until relatively recently dominated the market. Corporate responsibility can however be at marked variance with government policy. The Bechtel Corporation in the US, for example, offered to build Brazil's enrichment plant (which would give it nuclear weapons capability), without any prior consultation with government and despite knowing it was government policy to prevent the sale of such technology to Brazil. West Germany knew that Bechtel had made this offer, in competition with West German bids, and saw

US moves to stop their Brazilian contract as an attempt to preserve US commercial interests. This perception was mainly responsible for West German intransigence over the deal, now going ahead.[42]

Dale Bridenbaugh, along with two other senior nuclear engineers with the US company General Electric (GE), resigned because 'we could no longer justify devoting our life's energy to the continued development and expansion of nuclear fission power, a system which we believe to be so dangerous as to threaten the very existence of life on this planet'.[43] Bridenbaugh complained of GE's attitude towards reactor sales to Israel and Egypt. As President, Richard Nixon made a Middle East tour and offered nuclear power stations to both these countries. Bridenbaugh writes: 'I came back and asked my boss how we rationalise these sales to countries at war with each other. He said that wasn't our responsibility'.[44]

Among the other nuclear exporting countries, France is of particular significance, not having signed the NPT, and having made a number of highly controversial deals. As we have seen, it played a major role in the Iraqi nuclear programme, but at the same time helped Israel build the reactor at Dimona from which Israeli nuclear weapons material is derived. Israeli and South African scientists have been present at French nuclear tests in the Pacific.[45] In 1976, France agreed to build a reprocessing plant for Pakistan but the deal was suspended through pressure from the US. There is evidence that the plant is now being built in secret.[46] Clearly, commercial interest is militating against proliferation controls.

For Canada, the reverse is occurring: politicians there have expressed fears that it is losing sales for its Candu reactor because of the high level of proliferation safeguards now demanded with any sale. Proliferation safeguards were tightened after the Indian nuclear test, the plutonium for which was supplied by their Canadian reactor. It seems that the attempt to make nuclear power a relatively safer technology will price it out of the energy market altogether.

Nuclear power and the third world

Energy systems for the third world, and consequently the whole proliferation debate, cannot be discussed without looking at its political and economic struggle against underdevelopment and dependency on the industrialised countries. There is a colossal imbalance in the control and use of world energy resources. The industrialised countries use 100 times more energy per capita than the developing countries. All the fuel used by the whole of the third world for all purposes is only slightly more than the amount of fuel burnt in vehicles in the West.

The world petroleum market is dominated by seven big multinational companies. Their main strategy has been to maximise profits, minimise risk and ensure plentiful supplies of cheap oil for the industrial countries. When the Organisation of Petroleum Exporting Countries (OPEC) took action in 1973 to gain control of their own resources and increase their share of the proceeds from oil exports, the era of cheap energy came to an end. The profits of multinational oil companies have not slumped. Far from it, they now make more profit each year than they did in every five-year period up to 1973.[47]

The pattern of trade in the third world is moulded by the multinationals' policies and is one of exploitation and deliberate underdevelopment. Oil provides on average over 60 per cent of the third world's energy, yet 92 of these countries are heavily dependent on oil imports, 64 relying on oil imports for 75 per cent of their commercial energy.[48] It is claimed that the third world has little oil and that it can never hope to develop the infrastructure for an indigenous oil industry. Therefore, the argument goes, the third world should go straight to developing solar and nuclear technology.

Yet the non-OPEC third world does have oil – a study commissioned by the World Bank indicated that at least 60 billion barrels could be produced,[49] and an investment of $60 billion could decrease oil imports to zero.[50] The potential is vast in comparison with third world needs. The problem lies with the multinationals, which have blocked any attempt to aid these countries in developing their own oil resources because oil production in the third world is more lucrative than anywhere else. To allow these countries the freedom to develop their own oil reserves would mean a huge slump in multinationals' profits and the spread of oil-producing technology to other underdeveloped nations, further reducing oil company, and western political, hegemony.

Since the events of 1973, there has been a steady and undercover takeover of solar and nuclear technology by oil multinationals in an attempt to gain control of what they consider will be the next generation of energy technology. Thus the third world is kept dependent on oil while the stage is being set for their future dependence on nuclear and solar energy.

It is against this background that the proliferation debate is joined. If the essence of the nuclear arms race is power, then the development, actual or threatened, of nuclear weapons is an attractive lever for powerless third world countries against industrial and oil-exporting states. The creation of an export-orientated nuclear industry has set up its own political dynamic: exporting countries sell nuclear technology, trying to shore up an uneconomic industry, while turning a blind eye to proliferation risks. The importing countries in turn see nuclear power as a means of gaining energy independence with the potential strategic advantages of nuclear weapons. It is not 'insanity' that drives third world countries to spend vast amounts on nuclear power and arms while people starve. It is just one result of the political and economic system that rests on the relations of dependence and power between the third world and the West. It is revealing to take a close look at which countries have invested in nuclear technology over the past ten years. The list reads like a 'Who's Who' of repressive and/or military regimes, among them Brazil, Argentina, Chile, South Africa, the Philippines and Indonesia. Western governments and multinationals are supplying nuclear technology, often with massive financial aid from such agencies as the World Bank, to countries with appalling attitudes to human rights and political freedom. The features which make nuclear power a threat to civil liberties are those which military regimes find attractive, quite apart from the military potential.

As yet, policy-makers in the third world seem less aware of the hazards of nuclear power that concern so many people in the West. It is not a question of denying the third world a valuable and much-needed energy source in wishing to halt the spread of civil nuclear technology, rather a case of recognising that there are better ways of meeting energy needs, and that problems of nuclear safety, waste disposal, economics and the threat of ultimate destruction through the spread of nuclear weapons mean that all nations would do better to forgo the nuclear option.

The final solution?

The International Fuel Cycle Evaluation (INFCE) was set up in 1977 in response to President Carter's restrictions on plutonium-based technologies, and his request to find technological solutions to the proliferation of nuclear weapons. Its final report, published in 1980, recognises that there are few satisfactory technological measures that can be taken to prevent proliferation: the solution must be 'political'.

Walter Marshall, now chairman of the UKAEA, is a prolific writer within the British nuclear industry on the subject of weapons proliferation, who participated in, and shares the view of INFCE. He argues that since there are many routes to nuclear weapons, not all of which involve plutonium, there should be no need to restrict the development of plutonium technologies – in this context mainly reprocessing and the fast breeder reactor. The proliferation problem demands a political solution and therefore nuclear power 'should not be saddled with problems which are political and are not actually related to nuclear power at all'.[51] Proliferation is thus made 'inevitable', and so nuclear power can be developed without bearing the onus of responsibility.

Marshall's approach is at best irresponsible. Of course, there are many different clandestine paths to acquiring nuclear weapons, but one cannot count some as 'safe' and others as 'unsafe' on the basis of a judgement about the likelihood of particular paths being followed. The fact that countries could use various enrichment technologies, research reactors, or the theft or supply of weapons-grade material itself to enable them to make nuclear weapons, does not make it any more or less acceptable to export power reactors, fast breeder reactors or reprocessing plants. As Amory and Hunter Lovins have argued:

> Collectively, both familiar and newly emerging routes to bombs imply that *every* form of *every* fissionable material in *every* nuclear fuel cycle can be used to make military bombs, either on its own or in combination with other ingredients made widely and innocently available by nuclear power.[52]

The fact that Pakistan, for example, appears from recent evidence to have been attempting to acquire weapon capability by one of two routes – either by reprocessing spent reactor fuel or by constructing an enrichment plant based on secret plans stolen from the Dutch plant at Almelo[53] – does not suggest that it is alright to trade in some forms of nuclear technology and not others.

Marshall is particularly keen to claim that the fast breeder fuel cycle is proliferation-resistant. He advocates allowing third world countries to operate nuclear reactors, while reprocessing, enrichment and fast reactor technology remain in the hands of 'responsible' industrialised countries. The fast reactor, he points out, can be used primarily as an 'incinerator' of plutonium. At the end of each refuelling cycle, as much as 10 per cent of the plutonium in the core will have been consumed, while the plutonium 'bred' in the surrounding blanket of uranium 238 could be fed into another fast reactor after reprocessing. He argues that if the fast reactor is not adopted, and hence the spent fuel from present reactors not reprocessed, the plutonium contained in the spent fuel will over some years become progressively more accessible as levels of radioactivity decline. In other words, not reprocessing and not adopting fast reactors will lead to 'Plutonium mines', in the form of spent fuel, scattered around the world 'in hundreds of locations'. Thus, says Marshall, 'the best non-proliferation policy (assuming we must have nuclear power), is to build fast reactors with commendable speed'.[54]

The argument, while bold, is full of holes. As the Lovinses point out, Marshall's preferred solution in avoiding 'plutonium mines' will create a vast 'plutonium river', turning much of the world into a 'plutonium flood plain'.[55] While some developing countries are moving towards FBR technology (including India, Pakistan and Brazil), the 'plutonium economy' of the industrialised countries will still be open to the threat of diversion by non-state groups, other states or by the state itself circumventing safeguards. Marshall also overlooks the fact that in order to separate plutonium from spent fuel, it is not absolutely necessary to have reprocessing on a commercial scale; nor does he take into account the possibility that reactor-grade plutonium can be successfully fabricated into a credible nuclear explosive. The notion of confining certain 'sensitive' parts of the nuclear fuel cycle to a limited number of 'safe' western countries is as dangerous as it is naive. Marshall's contention smacks of neo-imperialism, maintains a fundamental form of world inequality, and will inevitably encourage more countries to try and illicitly acquire what the paternalistic West will not let them have. It will understandably reinforce third world perceptions of injustice, and as such increase the tensions between the developed and developing countries. Crucially, Marshall's barely explicit assumption – that some form of nuclear power is necessary – enables him to pursue a seemingly overwhelming logic which is actually flawed at root. Of course if one takes for granted the continuation of current types of reactors, the total amount of plutonium in existence will rise inexorably. Plutonium does not exist before it is created in a reactor. Equally, if the world's dependence on *any kind* of nuclear reactor were to be phased out, the production of plutonium would come to an absolute halt. Thus the best non-proliferation policy is to abandon all forms of nuclear power with commendable speed.

4.

Towards the Nuclear State

Writing in the magazine *Foreign Affairs* in 1953, J. Robert Oppenheimer – the man who organised the construction of America's first atomic bombs – described how a senior officer in US Air Defence Command had once said that it was not policy to protect US civilians from a nuclear attack. 'Such follies', observed Oppenheimer, 'can only occur when even the men who know the facts can find no one to talk to about them, when the facts are too secret for discussion, and thus, for thought'.

A year later, in one of the most disgraceful episodes in atomic history, following a four-week hearing under Chairman Gordon Gray, the US Atomic Energy Commission (USAEC) decided to remove Oppenheimer's security clearance. After devoting many years to working at Los Alamos on the Manhattan Project, Oppenheimer's future career was in ruins. A 'blank wall' between him and any new information on atomic weapons was permanently maintained. From being a national hero with an important influence inside the government, he became a political outcast. Personally, this manifestation of official mistrust took a heavy toll: photographs and newsreels featuring Oppenheimer after his ordeal show a man much changed, tired, older and more indifferent to the world. He never regained his security clearance, although before his death in 1967 he was given partial rehabilitation in the form of a USAEC award for his services.

The charges against Oppenheimer, raised in the era of McCarthyism, related mainly to his flirtation with communism in the 1930s: yet the Gray hearing concluded that he was 'a loyal citizen'. For almost all the period 1942-55 covering the Manhattan Project, Oppenheimer was subject to a rare degree of surveillance by the FBI: he was constantly followed, his phone was tapped, his mail opened and his offices and homes bugged. During the USAEC hearing the prosecution made extensive use of the immense FBI files on Oppenheimer – information not available to his defence.

It has also been alleged that discussions between Oppenheimer and his legal counsel prior to the hearing were bugged and made available to the prosecution. In spite of such extensive surveillance, no proof of any links with the Communist Party, or with Russia ever emerged. One area, however, where the hearing did criticise Oppenheimer was on his publicly-voiced opposition to US development of the hydrogen bomb. As chairman of the General Advisory Council to the USAEC, he had been largely responsible for the committee's recommendation not to proceed with the H-bomb – a move he believed would begin an unstoppable nuclear arms race. The Gray hearing concluded that Oppenheimer's position had meant that 'the security interests of the United States were affected'.

Peter Goodchild's lucid biography of Oppenheimer[1] draws the disturbing conclusion that the hearing 'was making a political assessment of Oppenheimer's negative attitude towards a particular weapons strategy.' Oppenheimer, in other words, was destroyed by the state, not because he was guilty of espionage, but simply because he was guilty of holding the wrong opinions and in a position to make those opinions felt.

The manifest injustice inflicted on 'the father of the atomic bomb' is characteristic of many of the problems encountered in the subsequent development of nuclear energy for both civil and military purposes. Oppenheimer's insight into the mistakes that flow from facts that are 'too secret for thought' is echoed by those who have analysed the decisions behind closed doors that led to the development of Britain's nuclear 'deterrent' and nuclear power programmes. The pall of secrecy which surrounds all matters nuclear has led to a lack of public accountability and incompetent decisions. The need for nuclear security has meant the erosion of basic civil liberties. Secrecy and security, combined with the innate characteristics of nuclear technology, are together threatening some of the basic tenets of a free and open democracy.

The case of Karen Silkwood

Oppenheimer was only the first – though perhaps the most famous – individual to be persecuted by the nuclear establishment. The tragic case of Karen Silkwood – now something of a cause célèbre in the anti-nuclear movement – and Trevor Brown, formerly a safety officer at Aldermaston, are more recent examples. Karen Silkwood was an official of the Oil, Chemical and Atomic Workers Union responsible for health and safety at Kerr McGee's plutonium plant in Cimarron, Oklahoma. She said she had evidence that the management at the plant was deliberately doctoring X-rays to disguise the fact that some plutonium fuel rods they produced were faulty. She also claimed that the company were guilty of gross violations of basic health and safety regulations. In November 1974, as she was on her way with documentary proof of her allegations to meet *New York Times* reporter David Burnham and a senior union official, her car was forced off the road and she was killed. Officials from Kerr McGee inspected the wreck at a local garage before David Burnham got to the scene: when he did arrive the manilla folder containing the proof of malpractice was missing. In May 1979 Oklahoma Federal Court awarded over ten million dollars damages to Silkwood's three children for the plutonium contamination she suffered while working at the plant.[2]

The case of Trevor Brown

In 1961 Trevor Brown, a chemist who had been working in weapons factories in the north of England since 1942, was asked by John Hill – later knighted and made Chairman of the UKAEA – to move to the Atomic Weapons Research Establishment (AWRE) at Aldermaston. He was told to use his managerial experience in working with dangerous materials to ensure that Aldermaston's poor safety record did not jeopardise its work on the fast reactor – a major part of AWRE's work for the civil programme at the time. As manager of fast reactor fuel development, he consistently demanded better safety data, proper training and access to outside experts on non-classified safety issues. One of his main complaints was that the fixed air samplers in use at Aldermaston to measure levels of atmospheric radioactivity were inadequate and needed to be supplemented by personal air samplers. In 1971 he took charge of the management of the wide spectrum of low, medium and high level radioactive wastes that are inevitably produced by military reactors and the manufacture of nuclear weapons, and persisted in his efforts to improve working conditions.

In 1973 he was elected as a Liberal county councillor for Newbury (East). He was approached in 1976 by several constituents – some of whom were themselves safety experts at Aldermaston – and asked to raise their concern about delays in implementing safety procedures with the local MP, Conservative Michael McNair Wilson. Soon afterwards Brown was accused by management of using typing pools at Aldermaston for council work – an allegation that was dropped when his staff association, the Institute of Professional Civil Servants, asked for supporting evidence.

After a decade of repeated requests, in 1977 Brown at last managed to get permission to introduce personal air samplers, which immediately showed disturbingly high levels of radioactivity. He discussed the readings with an expert from the National Radiological Protection Board who explained that internationally accepted regulations for the safe handling of plutonium appeared not to have been applied at Aldermaston.

Concern amongst staff over safety conditions mounted. Brown, meanwhile, was inexplicably refused permission to attend council meetings during worktime and was forced to appeal to the Industrial Tribunal, which subsequently upheld his right to represent his constituents by attendance. His superintending engineer for 1971-76 offered to testify on his behalf but was 'instructed' by a senior Aldermaston official to change his mind. In August 1978 it was announced that all work involving radioactivity at Aldermaston had ceased and ten buildings were closed pending an official inquiry into safety conditions at the site. After being for the first time subjected to whole-body monitoring, three workers were found to have between two and four times the internationally permitted levels of plutonium in their lungs. The report of the inquiry by Sir Edward Pochin largely upheld the criticisms made by Brown and his colleagues. Pochin said that levels of atmospheric contamination 'commonly exceeded' maximum limits, health measures at the plant were of 'borderline adequacy' and that there were 'serious deficiencies' in staffing. He urged a range of reforms such as increasing staff, improving training and better procedures.[3] At this point Brown says he was actually told that the delays in implementing safety procedures would be blamed on him.

In March 1980, still concerned about safety, Brown agreed to speak as a county councillor on the BBC Newsnight programme 'Is Aldermaston Safe?'. In the event he spoke just a few sentences describing what he had done and agreeing that 'an obsession with secrecy had possibly lowered safety standards'. The Aldermaston management, saying that he had been refused permission to appear on television (although later admitting that he had not revealed any information that was not already public knowledge), held a disciplinary tribunal under the chairmanship of AWRE Secretary Donald Hanson. In November 1980, Mr Brown was given a 'severe reprimand' on the grounds that as a civil servant he had been guilty of the 'public expression of views on official matters' and was threatened that 'the consequences could be most serious' in the event of a repetition. At the same time the Director of Aldermaston, Mr C.C. Fielding, told the House of Commons Defence Committee that five of the ten buildings shut down may never be fully re-opened, and there were allegations in the press that some of Pochin's recommendations had not been fully implemented.[4] Mr Brown was subsequently passed over for promotion and forced, by the threat of being moved to another area, to retire seven years early in April 1981.

In short, a senior scientist whose concern for safety at Britain's main atomic weapons facility led to and was vindicated by an official high-level inquiry, far from being rewarded for his services, has been harassed and victimised. It has been calculated that his damaged career and enforced retirement have cost him over £100,000 in income. Trevor Brown can be forgiven for indulging in a bitter speculative afterthought: 'I wonder whether I would not have done better had I been an upper-class spy rather than a working-class patriotic scientist.'[5]

Official secrecy

The history of the development of Britain's nuclear weapons and nuclear power programmes is dominated by an obsessive concern for secrecy. Within the secretive mode of British government that has become the norm, nuclear decision-making is one of the main areas where we can clearly see the damage that can be wrought by too little public accountability. The UKAEA's official historian, Professor Margaret Gowing, when asked to give a public lecture in 1978, chose the subject of atomic secrecy, about which she has strong feelings.[6] She points out that during the second world war, atomic energy was never discussed in the small war cabinet, and the Deputy Prime Minister Mr Attlee, the service ministers and the Chiefs of Staff knew 'almost nothing at all about it': such secrecy, she says, 'distorted constitutional government in Britain'. When Clement Attlee took charge of a new Labour government, just ten days prior to Hiroshima, he became 'obsessively secretive', ensuring that the Cabinet as a whole was completely excluded from major atomic decision-making. Gowing is disparaging about how decisions were taken: 'a small inner ring of senior ministers took decisions in a confusing number of *ad hoc* committees with science fiction titles, which never reported to the Cabinet'. Extraordinarily, quasi-ministerial responsibility for atomic energy continued to be vested in the war-time minister Sir John Anderson, after he had moved out of government to the opposition front bench.

Gowing is especially scathing about Attlee, saying that his:

> personal atomic initiative was mainly limited to stopping the release of almost any information about Britain's project. He sent a stream of tart personal minutes objecting to visits to unclassified areas of Harwell and the publication of the most innocuous material.

Ernest Bevin was apparently 'equally emphatic', thus ensuring that the very minimum of information was given to parliament and the press. The most crucial decision of all – to make Britain's first atomic bomb and hence ensure the continuation of the nuclear arms race started by the US – was taken in such deep secrecy that even those most affected never knew. An *ad hoc* meeting of just six ministers in January 1947 took the decision – but Christopher Hinton and William Penney, who were actually in charge of designing and building the bomb factories and the bombs, had never heard of this meeting until told of it 25 years later by Margaret Gowing. Winston Churchill returned to office in 1951 and maintained, according to Gowing, an 'equally restrictive secrecy'. Inevitably, the infatuation with secrecy carried over into the growing civil side of the nuclear industry and, according to Gowing again, 'prevented any clear public understanding of nuclear power'.

There is a long, inglorious list, stretching over the last three decades, of key governmental reports and documents on nuclear matters that have never seen the light of day.

* A paper produced by the government's chief adviser on defence research policy Sir Henry Tizard in 1949, apparently arguing against Britain's adoption of an independent nuclear 'deterrent', has not been published, even though such papers are usually available after 30 years, and in spite of the fact that Margaret Gowing seems to have read it.

* The full report, compiled under the chairmanship of Sir Alexander Fleck, on the 1957 fire at the Windscale no. 1 pile has never been published, although a truncated summary which blames an unnamed operator is available.

* The report of the Powell Committee, which was set up under the auspices of the Cabinet in 1962 to study the economics of nuclear power and coal, and the various possible reactor types, and which formed the basis of subsequent government decisions, has never been published. Prime Ministers Harold MacMillan in 1963 and Sir Alec Douglas-Home in 1964 refused to reveal its remit or its conclusions: Lord Carrington defended their policy on the grounds that the committee was a 'high-powered one – part of the confidential machinery of government'.

* The report of the Vinter Committee set up by the government in 1970 under Peter Vinter, a senior civil servant, to study the choice of reactor systems has never been published – it was even refused to the House of Commons Select Committee on Science and Technology in 1972.

* The report on the need for the second advanced gas-cooled reactor programme (Torness and Heysham) compiled in 1980 for the government by the Central

Policy Review Staff, the official 'think tank', has not been published or made available to the House of Commons Select Committee on Energy who thought this 'most regrettable'.

Professor Roger Williams in his important study of Britain's nuclear power decisions points out that all the main decisions on reactor choice were firmly based on much earlier and 'exclusively internal' decisions by the UKAEA.[7] He castigates such lack of openness and accountability as 'grotesquely inadequate, when millions, even billions of public money are at stake' and attributes the 'form, severity and chronic character' of the many technological and organisational problems that have beset the nuclear industry to the 'particular closed system in which they arose'.

If secrecy on the civil side is inhibiting, on the military side it is positively claustrophobic. UKAEA Chairman Sir John Hill rounded off his press conference launching the organisation's 16th annual report in 1970 – a time when he was still responsible for all atomic weapons research – by remarking briskly, 'I should say something of Aldermaston. The defence work there . . . is all highly classified and I can tell you nothing of it.'

A wide range of information that would have been useful in the writing of this book was likewise not publicly available. A whole series of parliamentary written questions for information on nuclear power and nuclear weapons asked in 1981 by Robin Cook MP, were given a polite brush off. The official risk assessments and safety manual that supported the government decision to allow the UKAEA to ship plutonium nitrate from Dounreay to Windscale were 'classified'. As to information on nuclear weapons research, the source of fissile material for Trident missiles, or the amounts of military waste: 'it has been the practice of successive governments not to divulge details'. When Robin Cook asked for the government simply to list topics relating to the civil nuclear programme which would be classified, Energy Under-Secretary Norman Lamont replied revealingly.

> Provision of information in the detail requested would represent a breach of classification. Some atomic energy information within the civil field is classified because it relates to the technologies for or the scale and cost of

production of those nuclear materials used in nuclear weapons; and to the storage and transport of such materials.[8]

In 1979 the then Energy Secretary Tony Benn revealed a number of important occasions on which he was aware that information on nuclear energy had been withheld from the minister responsible and the Cabinet by the UKAEA. These included knowledge of the 1957 nuclear disaster in Russia, the disappearance of a shipload of 200 tons of uranium in 1968, and the signing in 1970 of the controversial uranium contract with Rio Tinto Zinc for the Rössing mine in Namibia.

Margaret Gowing, unlike Tony Benn, looking back over the whole period of nuclear development, accuses ministers of both major parties of being far more restrictive on nuclear information than their civil servants. In sum she declares that the British government's nuclear policy has historically been 'largely irrational' in its relations to parliament, the press and the public. This situation seems unlikely to change. Leaked Cabinet committee minutes of October 1979, reveal that the government was unwilling to engage in too much public discussion, favouring a 'low profile approach' in the presentation of their decision to press ahead with a large nuclear power programme.[9]

The loss of civil liberties

An inevitable result of nuclear expansion is the need for heavy security which can and does lead to an attack on fundamental civil liberties – an attack that was felt in acute form by Oppenheimer, Silkwood and Brown. Prophetically, the Conservative Minister of Works in 1954, Sir David Eccles, put his finger on the problem when defending his government's plans to transfer work on atomic energy to the soon-to-be established UKAEA:

> The pity is that for us it is so hard to disentangle the innocent from the dangerous and the civil from the military . . . Thus we are bound to investigate the harmless man's background, and to take precautions about him, as though he were working on the weapons programme. That is why . . . the Official Secrets Act is applied to all the staff of the Authority and why the screening of individuals must continue.[10]

UKAEA staff are still covered by the Official Secrets Act, as are employees of BNFL, the Nuclear Installations Inspectorate and Department of Energy officials. Before anyone is employed by BNFL or the UKAEA they are 'positively vetted', a process which involves a rigorous investigation of the personal lives of individuals by security officers, and a five yearly review of political associations.

According to former UKAEA Chairman Sir John Hill, security at the 'more sensitive' nuclear power sites such as Windscale is 'still treated as if they were defence establishments'.[11] The UKAEA run their own special police force which in 1976 was granted unique powers to carry arms including machine guns, to engage in 'hot pursuit' of suspected persons and to arrest on suspicion. The police are deployed on UKAEA sites at Dounreay, Harwell, Winfrith and its London headquarters, and at BNFL's Capenhurst, Chapelcross, Springfields, Risley and Windscale sites – all establishments with military connections. They bear arms when accompanying the movement of fissile material between sites (such as plutonium nitrate between Dounreay and Windscale) and are trained in the use of riot gas. Annual public expenditure on the force during its first five years more than trebled to over £6 million in 1980-81, while its complement nearly doubled to over 600. Up to 1980 a total of 19 complaints were made against the special constables and 28 officers were disciplined. Predictably, the annual report of its chief constable is a 'classified document'.[12] The constables are only indirectly accountable to parliament via the UKAEA Chairman and the Secretary of State for Energy.

Fear of the appalling consequences that could result from the theft of plutonium and its use in the construction of crude atomic weapons or its dispersal into the atmosphere, has prompted many observers to suggest that the preventative measures that will be taken by the security services are bound to be draconian.[13] There is a real dilemma here: on the one hand the risk, however remote, of the illicit use of plutonium is so horrifying that virtually any measures that would help to prevent such an occurrence could be justified; but on the other hand there is no doubt that many such measures represent an increasingly worrying infringement of the civil liberties of many people.

The much-quoted Royal Commission on Environmental

Pollution's 1976 report on nuclear power emphasises precisely this point:

> What is most to be feared is an insidious growth in surveillance in response to a growing threat as the amount of plutonium in existence and familarity with its properties increases, and the possibility that a single serious incident in the future might bring a realisation of the need to increase security measures and surveillance to a degree that would be regarded as wholly unacceptable, but which could not then be avoided because of the extent of our dependence on plutonium for energy supplies.[14]

The dilemma arises precisely because plutonium is by nature ambiguous – it can be used to make atomic bombs just as easily as it can be used to power fast reactors.

A further problem relates to the growing disillusionment over the supposed impartiality of public inquiries into nuclear issues. The report on the 1977 Windscale Inquiry (which ignored much of the objectors' case), the 1980 inquiries in Ayr and Newcastle into proposals to test-drill for research into nuclear waste dumping sites, and the 1981 inquiry into NATO's plans to expand Stornoway airport in the Western Isles, have all been greeted with widespread cynicism. Writing in 1976, Flood and Grove-White[15] predicted that the role of the Secretary of State as original initiator and ultimate arbiter of any nuclear proposal would cause objectors to see the situation as 'inequitable', and could lead to civil disobedience: within two years, in the first direct action against civil nuclear power in Britain, 39 people were arrested for trying to prevent the start of work on the site for the proposed Torness nuclear station in East Lothian – the subject of a very limited planning inquiry in 1974. It is unlikely that future nuclear inquiries involving pressurised water reactors or fast reactors will re-establish faith in the system. Brian Sedgemore, who was Parliamentary Private Secretary to Tony Benn when he was Secretary of State for Energy between 1974 and 1979, recalls how UKAEA Chairman Sir John Hill in pressing Benn for an early start on the first commercial fast reactor following the promised inquiry, 'almost unwittingly has described an inexorable process leading to a certain conclusion'.[16] It is, Sedgemore suggests, a 'historical inevitability' that the Cabinet, regardless of the results of any public inquiry, will end up rubber-stamping the decision to build a commercial fast reactor.

There is also concern surrounding the effect that nuclear power could have, and already is having, in restricting trade union rights to information and to strike for better conditions. The 1977 unofficial Windscale strike, in which the Labour government's threat of bringing in troops to ensure the safety of the plant played a part in forcing the men back to work, is a worrying precedent.[17] There is a clear conflict between the need for public safety and the need to allow effective industrial action. Safety and security considerations are likely to be increasingly used in attempts to reduce the bargaining power of nuclear workers.[18]

The UKAEA's special autonomy

When the UKAEA was set up in 1954 it was recognised as a very unusual organisation. One Labour MP commented that:

> if the government were intending to design a framework for the overall control of atomic energy they could not possibly have thought of a framework under which it would be more difficult to ensure public accountability and proper parliamentary control.[19]

The UKAEA was to be something between a government department and a nationalised industry, a kind of semi-independent arm of the government machine, which reported directly to a minister of high Cabinet rank. According to Roger Williams, this unique position:

> reinforced by the prestige accruing to the AEA from the success of the military project and further projected by the esoteric nature of the authority's concerns, was to confer on them a rather special autonomy.[20]

The fact that the organisation was then still entirely responsible for both the military and civil aspects of the embryonic nuclear industry, also provoked opposition. One of the reasons Labour opposed the setting up of the UKAEA was, according to left-wing MP Emrys Hughes, because the minister was 'being given a blank cheque to manufacture atom bombs and hydrogen bombs'.[21]

For some within the industry the UKAEA's 'rather special autonomy' did not go far enough. Writing in 1976, after 'two decades of nuclear confusion', Sir Christopher Hinton complained that Britain needed a more 'autocratic organisation' suggesting that otherwise we might as well not bother with reactor development at all.[22]

The Commons Select Committee on Energy in 1981 trenchantly criticised the UKAEA for a catalogue of bad advice on previous reactor programmes and suggested that the official view that it was 'the principal adviser to the British government and CEGB [Central Electricity Generating Board] on all nuclear matters' was outdated.[23] The committee recommended that the UKAEA should not be directly involved in the ordinary reactor programme. They also pointed out that the Department of Energy, having insufficient atomic experts of their own, are ill-equipped to provide a proper check on nuclear industry activity. Some UKAEA senior officials appear to have abused their positions of influence. Sedgemore recounts his amazement at discovering that Dr Walter Marshall at the same time as being Chief Scientist at the Department of Energy and Deputy Chairman of the UKAEA, was also acting as safety adviser to the Shah of Iran's nuclear programme.[24] Marshall had actually been talking to the Iranian Foreign Minister about the possibility of Iran purchasing 20 pressurised water reactors (PWRs) from Britain. This deal was dependent on Britain adopting PWRs, yet was being discussed before the British government had even agreed to authorise the manufacture of a single PWR. What Sedgemore omits to mention about Marshall is that he was also Chairman of the Advisory Council on Research and Development for Fuel and Power, and responsible for the main government report on a possible rival to nuclear power, combined heat and power. In 1981, he became Chairman of the UKAEA.

The UKAEA is of course only one part of the chain of nuclear decision-making. Sedgemore describes the attempts in 1977 by the civil servants at the Department of Energy led by the Permanent Secretary Sir Jack Rampton, to subvert ministerial power on the question of future choice of reactors.[25] Rampton and his colleagues, in alliance with private industry (notably Sir Arnold Weinstock's General Electric Company (GEC)) mounted a fierce campaign in favour of a massive £20 billion PWR programme and poured scorn on the idea of relying on advanced gas-cooled reactors (AGRs) in the future. In what, according to Sedgemore, had 'all the makings of a public scandal', the civil servants circumvented, misled and manoeuvred in an attempt to get Cabinet approval for their PWR programme, against the advice of Energy Minister Tony Benn. Indeed Sedgemore says that 'the tactics were . . . such as to suggest the disappearance of that central core of integrity which once characterised the civil service machine'. In the end Benn won the battle and in January 1977 announced a programme for two AGR stations at Torness in East Lothian and Heysham near Lancaster. The civil servants, however, had the last laugh in more ways than one. In the final week prior to the May 1979 general election, Benn, acting as Energy Secretary, asked his private office to send a memo to UKAEA Chairman Sir John Hill asking him to suspend work on the PWR pending a full report on the implications of the Three Mile Island accident. Sir Jack Rampton, saying that Benn did not have the authority, simply refused to send it. In December 1979 the newly-elected Conservative government announced a £15 billion, 15,000 megawatt nuclear power programme, likely to be based primarily on PWRs. Rampton and his cohorts appear at last to have won a famous victory.

It is the link-ups between the UKAEA, BNFL, the electricity boards, the largely private reactor building industry dominated by GEC and Westinghouse, and senior civil servants, which together form the nuclear power lobby. Benn gained a rare insight into their combined strength: 'In my political life I have never known such a well-organised scientific, industrial and technical lobby as the nuclear power lobby'.[26] But they are themselves part of a much larger complex, encompassing the development and production of nuclear and other weapons.

Shared characteristics

Many of the factors that govern nuclear power and weapons decision-making are the same. Both technologies are exceedingly complex, needing long lead times from design to operation.

Reactors and weapons can typically take up to or more than ten years to move from ideas to working prototypes to finished products. Their technical sophistication is only fully understood by a relatively small number of highly-qualified 'expert' scientists and engineers who form an elite with a unique influence on government. Nuclear technologies are highly capital-intensive, demanding huge initial sums of money: £15 billion (1980 prices) for the government's nuclear power programme and at least £6 billion (1981 prices) for Trident. Conversely, they are not very labour-intensive, being amongst the most expensive methods available of creating employment. Both nuclear power and weapons are developed in conditions of deep secrecy, with decisions being taken behind closed doors by a small handful of powerful individuals and then revealed to an unsuspecting parliament and public. The nuclear power programme announced in 1979, rubber-stamped by the Cabinet, was not debated in the House of Commons until early 1982, while the £1 billion Chevaline programme to produce a new generation of nuclear warheads in place of Polaris was carried out for four years, mostly under a Labour government, before it was publicly admitted.

All these characteristics mean that nuclear technologies cohabit comfortably with large-scale centralised bureaucracies run by the state in conjunction with a few large private companies. The technocratic nature of nuclear technology reflects the hierarchical nature of the society that produced it and vice versa. Capitalist and state-capitalist relations of production are bound to lead to the introduction of machines that depend on the few controlling the many, such machines in turn strengthening existing inequalities. Society determines technology; then technology determines social and political progress; then society determines technology – and so on.[27] Nuclear developments, bolstered by a scientific elite and surrounded by an impenetrable jargon, secretly swallow immense amounts of money so that by the time the public realises what is happening, more nuclear 'progress' has become seemingly inevitable.

Nuclear technologies have a formidable technical and institutional momentum. Margaret Gowing has pointed out how in Britain's embryonic atomic project in 1949:

> the extraordinary collection of gifted scientists and engineers had developed its own momentum and its very existence had almost become the reason for its existence.[28]

Nuclear analyst John Simpson, in his evidence to the 1981 Commons Defence Committee, points out that Britain has built up considerable knowledge of ballistic missile warhead and guidance technology, which alongside decisions to commence tritium production at Chapelcross, to increase the production of enriched uranium at Capenhurst, and to develop a new submarine reactor at HMS Vulcan, provide an enormous impetus for the introduction of the Trident system. He concludes that the pressures in favour of Trident 'have now acquired a momentum of their own which makes it very difficult to question the functional benefits of such a course of action'.[29]

Towards the Nuclear State

Professor Stuart Hall's eloquent analysis takes the argument on a crucial stage. He suggests that the development of nuclear weapons systems with their accompanying network of bureaucracies has frozen society's capacity for social and political change. Moves towards an open and free democracy in any country are simply incompatible with an aggessive nuclear 'defence' policy. A nuclear-armed state is of necessity a state with no effective dissent, where the management of information is at its most intense. In sum:

> Nuclear weapons have had the effect of deepening the authoritarian content of political life within British society. Indeed in recent years we have seen the mutual reinforcement of the drive and drift towards the strong state inside, with its equivalent, the armed garrison state, outside.[30]

It is no coincidence that those countries who aspire to become nuclear powers tend to be governed by autocratic, often military establishments. Hall's basic thesis finds many echoes amongst others who have studied nuclear power and nuclear weapons issues. E.P. Thompson, for example, in expanding on his argument that 'civil liberties and 250 cruise missiles cannot coexist in this island together' has argued, perhaps in a bleak moment, that the era of identity cards, mass surveillance, habitual political trials, and large-scale state repression is just around the corner. He links nuclear-inspired authoritarianism to other perceived attacks on civil liberties – the decay of our jury system via jury vetting, the overtly political and increasingly brutal role of the police, telephone tapping, the management of opinion via state or corporation manipulation of the media, and the attack on trade union rights. Soon 'the British people will look back nostalgically and wonder where their constitution has gone'.[31] Thompson carries his argument further with a description of the corrupting influence on societies east and west of the nuclear arms race. The habit of Soviet/US opposition, and the doctrine of the (ever unstable) nuclear 'balance' has become part of the industrial and economic structure of both countries. On both sides, the power of the military industrial complex and its attached scientists is growing, accompanied by the management of opinion and the suppression of dissent. The logic of the cold war has become convenient to the ruling cliques of the superpowers in order to justify their privileges and high spending, and to control their satellite states. The military and political establishments have become locked into a degenerative process on course for mutual extermination.[32]

Walt Patterson, in his analysis of Britain's drift towards what he terms the 'fissile society', identifies the closed nature of nuclear decision-making as the 'inner sanctum' effect. If this continues to prevail and Britain becomes increasingly dependent on nuclear electricity:

> the stage will be set for the insidious establishment of an electro-nuclear technical oligarchy, exercising a fundamental influence on planning, finance and employment.[33]

Robert Jungk, the German writer, says that the 'nuclear gamblers and their aides are ready to sacrifice democracy in favour of a new hierarchical order' which he terms the 'nuclear state'.[34]

The development and expansion of nuclear power and nuclear weapons imply a level of secrecy, of security and of centralisation that threatens the free and democratic way of life. More people, like Oppenheimer, Silkwood and Brown, will be harassed, victimised, wronged and perhaps killed. The authoritarian trends in our society will be critically reinforced by the growth of a nuclear-powered nuclear-armed state. That is the seemingly inexorable course on which we are set. But it is not an inevitable path: perhaps we can still choose an alternative. Theoreticians are renowned for obscuring understanding by jargon and at the same time oversimplifying issues by positing unrealistic choices. Yet such choices, when offered, can help to clear our vision as to the right steps forward. Last century Karl Marx suggested that the choice the world had to face was 'socialism or barbarism,' Ivan Illich declares that now our choice is between a form of technocratic managerial fascism, or the reconstruction of society on the basis of 'conviviality', which he defines as a state where 'technologies serve politically inter-related individuals rather than managers'.[35] Whether one accepts Illich's precise definitions or not is irrelevant. Clearly the urgent task is to explore, openly and constructively, how we can work against the nuclear state to shift the odds back in favour of the survival of democracy, and, perhaps, the survival of the human race.

5.

Breaking the Nuclear Chain

> The search for practical ways to stop and even to reverse proliferation – the transcendent threat of our age – leads by inexorable logic to the necessity of phasing out nuclear power, as part of a coherent package of policies addressing both the vertical and horizontal spread of bombs.
>
> Amory Lovins and Hunter Lovins, 1981.

At the end of October 1981, the longest non-violent direct action against nuclear power in Britain ended. A group of protestors, after a 170-day occupation of a potential nuclear power station site at Luxulyan in Cornwall and a protracted legal battle, decided to leave the site and allow the Central Electricity Generating Board (CEGB) to commence survey work. The protest, according to the CEGB, had delayed work for five months and had cost the board over £130,000. The Luxulyan action – well organised and crucially dependent on local support – was the latest in a long tradition of civil disobedience against both civil and military nuclear developments.

The previous month in the United States, after a long campaign, 1,500 supporters of the Abalone Alliance were arrested – many of them twice – for attempting to blockade the Diablo Canyon nuclear power plant in California to prevent it from starting up. Following the blockade, the commissioning of the plant was indefinitely delayed as major flaws in its construction were discovered. Over recent years in Britain there have been a series of non-violent direct actions against the construction of a nuclear power station at Torness in East Lothian and against the dumping of nuclear waste at sea and on land. The government's plans to expand the Coulport nuclear base on the Clyde to accommodate the Trident missile system have already met with direct action, and more is promised. These protests echo those of the Committee of 100 in the 1960s, who faced arrest by mass 'sit-downs' in protest against nuclear weapons. The Committee had an at times uneasy alliance with the 'mainstream' protest group, the Campaign for Nuclear Disarmament (CND). Similarly, the relationship amongst groups opposed to nuclear power, between those concerned to act within the law and those prepared to go outside the law, has not always been harmonious.

In any constructive analysis such tensions are irrelevant. Movements that mean to change government policy through changes in public opinion need to attract a broad range of people and adopt many different tactics. Symbolic direct action against a particular development is useless unless it is accompanied by growing political pressure: parliamentary lobbying unaccompanied by a wider movement is unlikely to have any effect. Those who believe that the government can be persuaded to abandon its nuclear technologies, and those who believe that it must be forced to do so, are really two strands of the same movement. The successful campaign depends upon a careful balance of the legal and the illegal, the parliamentary and the extra-parliamentary, judged and implemented in accordance with the climate of public opinion. Decisions can be changed and policies reversed only by a combination of political will and public action.

The anti-nuclear movement in Britain is diverse. It encompasses the whole spectrum of political opinion, as well as the blithely non-political. But there is a confusion over precisely what it means to be 'anti-nuclear'. Does it mean to oppose Britain's possession of nuclear weapons, or its use of nuclear power to produce electricity, or both? The confusion is reflected in the stances adopted in the past. During the founding and dramatic growth of CND in the late 1950s and early 1960s the issue of nuclear power was barely mentioned. Some of those prominent in the peace movement were even enthusiastic about the use of 'atoms for peace'. The emergence in the 1970s of a campaign against nuclear power was, at least initially, part of a wider concern about the destruction of the environment and the depletion of natural resources. The ultimate ecological catastrophe, a nuclear holocaust, was not considered as a campaigning issue, reflecting the lack of public concern. By the early 1980s perceptions had changed. CND had, after some controversy, agreed a policy that encompassed opposition to nuclear power, and several anti-nuclear power groups had broadened their remit to include opposition to nuclear weapons. The theory of 'deterrence' was fast losing credibility after the emergence of nuclear war-fighting doctrines which explicitly accepted the possibility of launching the first strike, thus rendering nuclear conflict more likely. The world seemed to be dominated by increasingly careless and bellicose leaders. Widespread fears about the safety of nuclear power were aroused by the accident in 1979 at the Three Mile Island nuclear power plant. Public concern over both nuclear issues was mounting dramatically. After demonstrations of over 10,000 people against nuclear power at Torness and in London, in October 1980 CND held its first national demonstration for six years. Over 100,000 people packed Trafalgar Square in London to protest against government decisions to accept cruise and deploy Trident missiles. By the following year CND had grown too big for Trafalgar Square: on 24 October 1981 at least 150,000 people – some estimates put the number at 250,000 – assembled in Hyde Park under the slogan 'Together we can stop the bomb'. Yet there is still misunderstanding. Many of those inclined to support CND, especially within the trade union and labour movement, still give their uncritical backing to the further development of nuclear power. In 1981 the Trades Union Congress and the Labour Party both passed clear unilateralist resolutions, yet maintained policies which supported nuclear power.

The continued belief in 'atoms for peace' is in part a legacy of the emotional revulsion prompted by the horrors of Hiroshima and Nagasaki. Scientists responsible for the first atomic bombs were understandably so appalled by the devastation that they became very anxious to demonstrate that there was some good to be had from their discovery. David Lilienthal, the first Chairman of the US Atomic Energy Commission, has recalled how there was, 'a conviction, and one that I fully shared, and tried to inculcate in others, that somehow or other the discovery that had produced so terrible a weapon simply had to have an important peaceful use.'[1]

The 'need' for nuclear power

Another reason for some people's reluctance to link the struggle against nuclear arms with the struggle against nuclear power is the idea that nuclear electricity is 'needed' to help meet Britain's energy requirements. The burden of evidence indicates that in fact this country could do without nuclear power and still maintain and improve the standard of living of its people.[2] The nuclear industry's case for the development of nuclear power is fatally flawed: it is based on unrealistic energy forecasts and warped economic criteria. In 1963 the industry was predicting that electricity demand would be higher in 1968 then they now think is likely for 1986. Department of Energy forecasts of future energy demand made in 1978 and 1979 rest on simple extrapolations of pre-1973 figures – before the oil crisis rocked the world energy market.[3] Due to exaggerated demand forecasts in the past the Central Electricity Generating Board and the South of Scotland Electricity Board in 1980 both had a large overcapacity of supply – respectively 29 per cent and 73 per cent. The economic case for nuclear as against coal-fired electricity has been shown to be based on unsound methodology. Several critics have redone the sums to reveal that coal-fired electricity is in fact substantially cheaper than the nuclear alternative.[4] The Central Electricity Generating Board's nuclear power programme was condemned by the Monopolies Commission in 1981 as it was , 'proposed on the basis of investment appraisals which are seriously defective and liable to mislead. We conclude that the Board's course of conduct in this regard operates against the public interest.'[5]

The Conservative government's enthusiasm for nuclear power is motivated less by economics and energy needs than by blatantly political considerations. The leaked Cabinet committee minutes describing a meeting in October 1979 on the government's nuclear power policy, state unequivocally that a major nuclear power programme 'would have the advantage of removing a substantial proportion of electricity production from the dangers of disruption by industrial action by coal miners or transport workers'.[6] For the Conservatives, nuclear power is another tool for diminishing the influence of the trade union movement.

Internationally, the nuclear power industry is in the midst of a massive slump: between 1977 and 1981 more nuclear reactors were cancelled than were ordered in the West.[7] In Britain the proposed advanced gas-cooled reactors (AGRs) at Torness and Heysham are the first to be ordered for over a decade. One of the main justifications publicly advanced by the industry and the government for building these two stations is not that they are needed to meet future electricity demand, but that they are necessary for the purposes of keeping the beleaguered industry alive. In 1981 the House of Commons Select Committee on

Energy concluded that 'there was undoubtedly a case for not ordering two AGRs'.[8] The Select Committee also delivered a fierce judgement on the industry's past record:

> Enormous past nuclear investments have had exceptionally low productivity; great resources have been used with little direct return and a serious net loss.[9]

After thousands of millions of pounds of investment over a quarter of a century, nuclear power provides less than two per cent of Britain's delivered energy.[10]

In spite of the huge imbalance of investment – between 1975 and 1980 Britain spent forty times as much on research into nuclear power as it did into alternative energy sources and energy conservation[11] – it is now clear that Britain could abandon nuclear power without any decline in its standard of living. Indeed, the International Institute for Environment and Development has estimated that the UK could plan for zero energy growth to the year 2025 with a threefold growth in the economy.[12] The key to such a strategy is to begin for the first time to match the quality and type of energy that people actually use with the quality and type of energy that can be produced. In practice this means, in the short term, relying upon a combination of the cleaner and more efficient use of fossil fuels and energy conservation. A wide range of job-creating measures could be introduced as part of an urgent programme to combat unemployment. Britain's vast coal reserves, which are expected to last for several centuries, could be used to fuel combined heat and power district heating schemes, designed to utilise the large amounts of heat usually wasted in electricity generation. Comprehensive building insulation and vehicle design changes, for example, could save substantial amounts of energy, yet the government has ignored the real potential of such measures. The Select Committee criticised the Department of Energy for having 'no clear idea of whether investing around £1,300 million in a single nuclear plant . . . is as cost effective as spending a similar sum to promote energy conservation'.[13] The Open University Energy Research Group has shown how we can at least double the efficiency with which we currently use fuels.[14] The former chairman of the government's Advisory Council on Energy Conservation, Sir William Hawthorne, has said that 'existing technology lavishly applied could almost halve our energy consumption'.[15]

In the longer term there is need to look for other alternatives. By the year 2000, given the right kind of investment decisions now, Britain could become increasingly reliant on the renewable technologies based on the sun, wind and waves. Solar energy, for example, could supplement and ultimately replace combined heat and power district heating schemes in supplying much of the country's space and water heating requirements which make up 40 per cent of end-use energy needs. By 1980 there were already 4-5,000 flat plate solar collectors installed in Britain and the market was booming. It has been estimated that, given a vigorous energy conservation programme, about ten per cent of our energy needs could come from renewable sources by the end of the century, and as much as 50 per cent by 2025. One authoritative Swedish study estimates that renewable energy could supply virtually all that country's needs by 2015.[16]

Towards complete disarmament

Nuclear power was born out of British and US war-time efforts to construct an atomic bomb. At crucial stages in its development, military priorities determined civil decisions. There are still deep structural links between nuclear electricity and warheads: many ostensibly civil nuclear sites perform key military functions. Following major strategic military decisions in Britain and the US, the unambiguously weapons-related activities carried out by the 'civil' nuclear industry are on the increase. Internationally the spread of nuclear power technologies is leading directly to the spread of nuclear weapons, encouraged by the illusion of a safeguards system. In Britain the growth of the military-industrial complex has been so centralised, so capital-intensive, so inflexible and so secretive that it now poses a threat to the continuation of democracy: we are drifting towards the nuclear state.

Nuclear power and nuclear weapons are not the same and they are not separate, but they are indissolubly linked. In franker moments even nuclear industry representatives will concede the basic point. UKAEA Chairman Sir John Hill admitted in 1979 that 'in the last analysis there is no such thing as the civil atom or the military atom'.[17] One man in a position to give a rare insight into the actual relationship between the two sides of the nuclear industry, former Energy Secretary Tony Benn, believes that 'civilian nuclear power is the public front for military nuclear weapons'.[18]

The proposals to expand Britain's nuclear arsenal with Trident and to accept US cruise missiles, and the plans to expand the country's nuclear power programme should be seen in the same context and simultaneously opposed. The nuclear industrial processes provide the basic materials and infrastructure necessary for nuclear weapons. Enrichment plants turn natural uranium into bombs-grade uranium, power stations turn uranium into plutonium and reprocessing plants separate the plutonium for use in nuclear warheads. Any country that has nuclear power will always have the capability to make nuclear weapons. Nuclear power technologies are the essential basis from which weapons states increase their stockpiles (vertical proliferation) and non-weapons states acquire nuclear capability (horizontal proliferation).

It is possible to envisage a form of nuclear disarmament in Britain which allowed the continuance of nuclear power. A British government could take a progressive series of decisions – the cancellation of Trident, the refusal of cruise missiles, the eviction of US nuclear bases and the closure of British nuclear bases – which would begin the urgent task of reversing the nuclear arms race. Presumably such a strategy would also permanently shut down the Atomic Weapons Research Establishment at Aldermaston and the bomb-construction factory at Burghfield. Yet, if we stop there, the disarmament process will be incomplete and ineffectual. If Britain maintains its nuclear power programme and carries on creating and extracting fissile material, it will still be able to export nuclear weapons ingredients to the United States. Any future government will always be in a position to construct new nuclear weapons *within a few days*. Nuclear disarmament which failed to include the abandonment of *all forms* of nuclear fission would be for ever uncertain. The only logical and consistent course of action is to scrap nuclear weapons and to close down the key industrial processes that gave birth to those weapons. Explicitly, this means the closure or non-completion of all Britain's 20 nuclear power stations and the permanent shutting-down of the fuel fabrication plant at Springfields, the enrichment plants at Capenhurst and the reprocessing plants at Windscale.

The implementation of such a radical policy of denuclearisation still leaves one difficult problem unsolved – what to do with the accumulated stockpiles of nuclear materials. The fissile material created since 1945 – though after some years it would become too contaminated to be used predictably as an explosive – would have to be destroyed. The tankfuls of radioactive waste and large quantities of radioactive rubble would, if left alone, remain harmful to life for centuries. Although virtually no analyst has addressed this problem, it seems that the only technically feasible method known of accelerating the natural decay process of such materials is to irradiate them in a nuclear reactor. In our complete disarmament strategy, it may thus be necessary to retain – at least for a while – a core of leading nuclear scientists to design and operate a single new type of reactor, for the sole purpose of neutralising nuclear materials.

For a truly nuclear-free future

The world in the early 1980s is a frightening place. World military expenditure escalates and increasingly sophisticated weapons are developed in an insane competition for strategic advantage. The total explosive power released in the second world war is now contained in single bombs that can fit beneath a bed.[19] US leaders drop casual hints that they can foresee Europe being used as a 'theatre' for a 'limited' nuclear war. The British Conservative government willingly acquiesces, professing surprise that the British people do not warm to the idea. Russia, fearful of a reduction in its sphere of influence, having invaded Afghanistan, makes threatening gestures towards Poland. Destabilising conflicts in the Middle East and Southern Africa simmer and threaten to boil over. In this context, more people are losing faith in the deteriorating doctrine of 'deterrence' and beginning to realise that a greater hope of survival may lie in a radical break from conventional wisdom. If one country voluntarily renounced its nuclear weapons, is there not a chance that its political example would jolt the world towards disarmament?

Perhaps more than anything else the campaign for a nuclear-free zone in Europe has captured the imagination of a generation anxious for survival. It is a new, constructive and potentially realisable objective. Yet unless such initiatives are firmly linked to the abandonment of nuclear power, unless all nuclear technologies are recognised as a potential weapons technologies, permanent and total disarmament will remain illusory.

Appendix 1:

Nuclear Power and Paths to the Bomb

There are two basic kinds of nuclear reactions: fission, in which atoms are split, and fusion, in which atoms are fused together.

Nuclear fission occurs when the nuclei (the centres) of certain atoms are bombarded by sub-atomic particles called neutrons. When the atom splits, a minute part of the atom's mass is converted into energy, according to Einstein's equation $E=mc^2$, where c is the speed of light, E is energy and m is mass. During fission, neutrons are released and, if the conditions are right, these can then go on to split other atoms and establish a chain reaction. This process is fundamental to both bombs and reactors. In a bomb, the energy is released in a very short time, creating an uncontrolled chain reaction and a massive explosive effect. In a nuclear reactor, the energy is released in a controlled fashion by regulating the amount of neutrons present. In all reactors except FBRs (i.e. 'thermal' reactors), a material that slows down neutrons – a moderator – is introduced into the reactor core.

A thermonuclear fusion weapon (hydrogen bomb) has a fission bomb (atom bomb) at its core, the heat from which is enough to cause the fusion of the heavy hydrogen (i.e. deuterium and/or tritium) packed around it. Bombs above 100 kilotons of TNT equivalent tend to be thermonuclear weapons. Fusion reactors would attempt to control this reaction, but since extremely high temperatures are involved, they are a distant prospect and may never be feasible.

Materials that readily undergo fission are called 'fissile'. Other substances are capable of being converted into fissile material, and are said to be 'fertile'. Some substances have different types, or 'isotopes' which have slightly different masses. The fissile material used to provide the explosive force for weapons has either been the isotope uranium 235 or plutonium 239. Neither of these is found in a usable form in nature. The Hiroshima bomb used uranium 235, the Nagasaki one plutonium 239. The countries that have tested thermonuclear weapons have initially used uranium 235 as the 'trigger', although subsequently plutonium has also been used, and probably plutonium mixed with uranium 235.

Stretching behind bombs and reactors is the nuclear fuel cycle – a chain of technological stages that have to be gone through before fuel can be made for power stations or material extracted for bombs.

The nuclear fuel cycle

Uranium mining

Uranium is the raw material for both bombs and power, eventually yielding both uranium 235 and plutonium 239. Mining operations devastate the areas where uranium is worked, as only a small proportion of the rock is uranium ore. The rock is crushed and the ore converted into uranium oxide, or yellowcake, for shipment. Many mines have displaced indigenous peoples, and all leave 'tailings' – huge mountains of useless crushed rock which are radioactive. For miners and the neighbouring populations, uranium mining is a severe health hazard.

Enrichment

Only 0.7 per cent of uranium ore is fissile uranium 235, the rest being uranium 238. Most reactors and all bombs require a higher percentage of uranium 235. The enrichment process yields higher concentrations of uranium 235 by exploiting the small difference in mass between the two isotopes. For reactor fuel, enrichment is to between 1.5 and 3 per cent. For bombs it is usually over 90 per cent, although over 50 per cent is considered a proliferation risk. The enrichment process is essentially the same for both bombs and reactors, and is the most energy intensive stage of the fuel cycle.

Nuclear power stations

In a nuclear power station, the reactor replaces the coal or oil furnace of a conventional power station. Instead of the energy release (in the form of heat) being produced by chemical combustion, nuclear fission supplies heat. (For a description of the different reactor types, see Walt Patterson's seminal book *Nuclear Power*, Penguin, 1980, pp. 42–86.) When uranium 238 is bombarded in a nuclear reactor, it is transformed into many different materials, including a new element, plutonium, which is fissile. The isotope plutonium 239 is initially created; but with longer bombardment by neutrons, plutonium 240 and 242 are created. These last two fission spontaneously, and thus plutonium produced in nuclear reactors (or 'reactor-grade plutonium') is said to be unsuitable for use in nuclear weapons as it makes them unstable. The distinction between 'reactor-grade' and 'weapons-grade' plutonium is, however, of doubtful validity.

Plutonium created in the reactor is mixed with a variety of 'waste' products which are highly radioactive and give off heat. This 'spent fuel' is removed from the reactor and transferred to a cooling pond, for a period of approximately 100 days. The time in the cooling ponds is necessary for the waste to lose some of its radioactivity and heat. The spent fuel (still highly radioactive) is then removed in heavily-shielded flasks by road and rail to a reprocessing plant.

Reprocessing

This involves stripping off the cladding surrounding the spent fuel, which is then dissolved in solvents, and uranium and plutonium are separated out for further use. Reprocessing to recover uranium for re-use in reactors is not proven to be economical. In Britain, reprocessing of spent fuel from the first generation Magnox reactors is essential because it cannot be stored safely, as the cladding corrodes and contaminates the storage vessel with radioactive caesium 137. Reprocessing is also 'essential', however, to recover the plutonium for weapons, or for use in the fast breeder reactor.

Fast breeder reactors

These reactors are designed to use plutonium, or a mixed fuel of plutonium and uranium, in their core. A 'blanket' of fertile uranium 238 is placed round the core (as an array of 'rods') and is changed into plutonium 239 by neutrons escaping from the fuel in the core. The 'blanket' can then be removed and reprocessed to give more plutonium for re-fabrication into fuel.

Waste disposal

The nuclear fuel cycle, like every industrial process, leaves behind waste. But unlike other industries, some of the waste from nuclear power and nuclear weapons programmes is highly radioactive, and therefore has to be isolated from all forms of life. Radioactive elements decay with time, but for some this period is extremely long: plutonium 239, for example, remains a hazard for 240,000 years. At present, waste from military and civil programmes is stored in 'temporary' silos awaiting a final solution to the problem of disposal. Current research is focused on the vitrification process, where the liquid waste is concentrated and then incorporated into glass blocks. One plan is to place these in temporary underground air-cooled stores until their heat decays to the point where they can be sealed in boreholes in granite rock. Another notion is to leave the waste to decay above ground and to put it underground after 50 or 100 years. Considerable uncertainty surrounds these plans: there is no guarantee that waste will not leach from the glass blocks out into groundwater and hence into drinking supplies. It is not surprising that research drilling for possible waste disposal sites has been blocked by the local population virtually everywhere drilling applications have been made. Wastes of lesser radioactivity are either buried on land, dumped at sea or released to the atmosphere.

Weapons manufacture

Plutonium from reprocessing and uranium from enrichment go to weapons establishments (in Britain, Aldermaston and Burghfield) where they are used for research or fabricated into nuclear weapons. Tritium – an essential component of thermonuclear weapons – is also required, and is produced by irradiation of lithium inside a reactor.

There is another fissile material – uranium 233 – which potentially could be used as bomb material or reactor fuel. Thorium 232 is the fertile material, and exists in deposits worldwide, but as yet the theory has not been translated into practice, as far as is known.

Appendix 2:

The Creation of Plutonium in Britain

1. In a parliamentary written answer on 3 March 1980, Energy Under-Secretary Norman Lamont said that the yield of plutonium per year from a Magnox station of 1,000 megawatts electrical capacity operating continuously would be 0.75 tonnes. On 29 October 1981 another parliamentary written answer made it clear that this figure was based on an annual average availability of between 74 and 75 per cent for a station with a gross installed capacity of 1,000 megawatts. Therefore 1 tonne of plutonium will be created by 8.76 million megawatt hours of Magnox operation.

2. According to a parliamentary written answer on 28 October 1981 from Lamont's successor David Mellor, Calder Hall and Chapelcross stations had generated totals of 37.261 and 37.645 million megawatt hours respectively up to the end of September 1981. Therefore we estimate that the two stations have together produced about 8.5 tonnes of plutonium.

3. According to another parliamentary written answer on 28 October 1981 from David Mellor, the total amount of electricity generated by Britain's nine other Magnox stations up to the end of September 1981 was 415.777 million megawatt hours. Therefore we estimate that they have produced about 47.5 tonnes of plutonium.

4. Thus the total amount of plutonium created by all Britain's Magnox reactors up to the end of September 1981 is about 56 tonnes.

5. According to a letter of 22 March 1982 to Robin Cook MP from Energy Under Secretary John Moore, at the end of 1981 there were 8.5 tonnes of plutonium in the fuel of civil Magnox reactors, 3.5 tonnes in fuel discharged but not yet reprocessed, 14.5 tonnes stored and 0.5 tonnes 'in process' at Windscale, 5.5 tonnes used in fast reactor research and 0.5 tonnes exported 'for civil purposes', giving a total of 33 tonnes. *Therefore there are over 20 tonnes of plutonium the existence of which has not been officially acknowledged.*

6. This is an underestimate of all the plutonium produced in Britain because:
    a) it does not take account of the plutonium produced in the two Windscale piles prior to 1957;
    b) it does not take account of any plutonium produced from other sources, such as Dounreay or other research or prototype civil or military reactors;
    c) it does not take account of the plutonium contained in the spent fuel from the advanced gas-cooled reactor stations.

Glossary of technical terms

Ballistic missile a missile that travels on free-fall trajectory after launch.
Blanket fuel elements surrounding the core in a fast breeder reactor, containing uranium 238 which is converted to plutonium by neutron bombardment.
Chain reaction a nucleus undergoes fission and releases neutrons which then go on to fission other nuclei, and hence fissioning and the release of neutrons multiply.
Cladding material covering nuclear fuel to protect it and keep in the radioactive products.
Coolant material transferring heat away from the reactor core. Different types of reactor use different coolants. Carbon dioxide gas, ordinary water, helium gas, heavy water and liquid sodium are the most used coolants.
Cooling pond deep tank of water into which spent fuel is discharged from the reactor.
Core central part of the reactor where the chain reaction occurs.
Critical nuclear material just capable of supporting a chain reaction is said to be 'critical', i.e. neutrons are captured and released at the same rate.
Decay disintegration of radioactive elements over time, releasing radiation.
Enrichment the process of increasing the concentration of the isotope uranium 235 in uranium beyond the 0.71 per cent contained in natural uranium.
Fast breeder reactor or fast reactor a reactor with no moderator, so the neutrons from the reaction are not slowed down (i.e. are 'fast' neutrons). It produces more fissile material than it consumes by 'breeding' fissile material in a blanket of fertile material.
Fertile material that can become fissile by capturing one or more neutrons.
Fissile material that will undergo fission if it captures a neutron.
Fission splitting of a heavy nucleus into two or more parts, releasing energy.
Fission product light nucleus formed by fission.
Fuel arrangement of fissile material in a reactor. Some reactors use natural uranium, others slightly enriched uranium (between 1-4 per cent of uranium 235), others (mainly reactors that do not produce power, or submarine reactors) use highly enriched uranium and others use plutonium.
Fusion merging of two light nuclei to make a heavier one, releasing energy.
Gas centrifuge uranium enrichment device by which heavier uranium 238 atoms are slightly separated from lighter uranium 235 atoms by centrifuging uranium hexafluoride gas. Full-scale plants use many thousands of centrifuges in a cascade.
Gas diffusion uranium enrichment process utilising the slight difference in the rate

of diffusion of uranium 235 and 238 atoms through a metallic membrane. Thousands of diffusion cells are used in a commercial plant.

Graphite black compacted crystalline carbon used as a moderator.

Heavy water isotopes of hydrogen, either deuterium (two mass units) or tritium (three mass units) combined with oxygen to make water.

Highly enriched uranium uranium in which the proportion of uranium 235 has been increased to 90 per cent or above.

Hot cell room with heavily shielded walls within which highly radioactive materials can be handled by remote control.

Irradiation time the length of time fuel spends in a reactor being bombarded by neutrons.

Isotope nuclei of the same chemical element differing in mass.

Laser enrichment separation of isotopes by selectively exciting one by laser.

Light water ordinary water, used as a coolant and as a moderator.

Load factor a measure of operating efficiency of a reactor. The ratio of total output of a reactor to its designed maximum capacity in a certain period.

Magnox name of the magnesium alloy fuel cladding in the first British nuclear power stations, and hence the name of that type of reactor.

Moderator material used to slow down neutrons in a reactor to enable them to be captured and allow fission. Common moderators are graphite, light water and heavy water.

Neutron particle in the nucleus (centre) of an atom, released during fission.

On-load refuelling replacement of reactor fuel while the reactor is still sustaining a chain reaction.

Pile name of original nuclear reactors, where 'piles' of uranium were cooled by gas or water, and moderated by graphite or water.

Radiation particles or energy formed by spontaneous decay of radioactive substances or during fission.

Radioactivity behaviour of a substance in which nuclei are undergoing transformation and emitting radiation, i.e. radioactivity produces radiation.

Reactor an arrangement to create and control a chain reaction.

Rem a unit for measuring radiation which takes into account the degree of harmful effects on biological tissue caused by each kind of radiation.

Reprocessing the chemical separation of irradiated nuclear fuel into plutonium, uranium and radioactive waste components.

Spent fuel fuel that has undergone a chain reaction and is nearing the point where it can no longer do so (as its fissile material has been transformed into other elements) and has thus been discharged from the reactor.

Spontaneous fission the breaking up of heavy nuclei without external initiation.

Thermonuclear fusion.

Yellowcake a mixture of uranium oxides, a yellow powder.

Select Bibliography

Nuclear power

Peter Bunyard, *Nuclear Britain*, New English Library 1981.
Robin Cook, *No Nukes!*, Fabian Society 1981.
Dave Elliott, *et al, The Politics of Nuclear Power*, Pluto Press 1978.
Nuclear Power and the Environment, Sixth Report of the Royal Commission on Environmental Pollution, Chairman Sir Brian Flowers, Cmnd. 6618, HMSO 1976.
Walter C. Patterson, *Nuclear Power*, Penguin 1980.
Martin Stott and Peter Taylor, *The Nuclear Controversy*, Town and Country Planning Association in association with Political Ecology Research Group 1980.

Nuclear weapons

Britain and the Bomb, New Statesman Report No. 3, 1981.
E. P. Thompson and Dan Smith (eds.), *Protest and Survive*, Penguin 1981.
John Cox, *Overkill: The story of modern weapons*, 3rd edition, Pelican 1980.
Sir Martin Ryle, *Towards the Nuclear Holocaust*, 2nd edition, Menard Press 1981.
Dan Smith, *The Defence of the Realm in the 1980s*, Croom Helm 1980.
Stockholm International Peace Research Institute (SIPRI), SIPRI Yearbook, *World Armaments and Disarmament*, annually since 1968–69.

Nuclear history

Duncan Burn, *Nuclear Power and the Energy Crisis*, Macmillan 1978.
Margaret Gowing, *Britain and Atomic Energy 1939–45*, Macmillan 1964.
Margaret Gowing, *Independence and Deterrence, Vol. 1 Policy Making*, Macmillan 1974.
Margaret Gowing, *Independence and Deterrence, Vol. 2 Policy Execution*, Macmillan 1974.
Roger Williams, *The Nuclear Power Decisions: British Policies 1953–78*, Croom Helm 1980.

Proliferation

Zdenek Cervenka and Barbara Rogers, *The Nuclear Axis*, Julian Friedmann 1978.

Elaine Davenport *et al*, *The Plumbat Affair*, Futura 1978.
Amory B. Lovins and L. Hunter Lovins, *Energy/War: Breaking the nuclear link*, San Francisco Friends of the Earth 1981.
Dan Smith, *South Africa's Nuclear Capability*, World Campaign against Military Nuclear Collaboration with South Africa 1980.
Albert Wohlstetter *et al*, *Swords from Ploughshares*, University of Chicago Press 1979.

The nuclear state

Robert Jungk, *The Nuclear State*, John Calder 1979.
Michael Flood and Robin Grove-White, *Nuclear Prospects: A comment on the individual, the state and nuclear power*, Friends of the Earth with the Council for the Protection of Rural England and the National Council for Civil Liberties 1976.
Missiles, Reactors and Civil Liberties: Against the nuclear state, Scottish Council for Civil Liberties 1981.
Walter C. Patterson, *The Fissile Society*, Earth Resources Research 1977.

Alternatives

David Dickson, *Alternative Technology and the Politics of Technical Change*, Futura 1974.
Gerald Leach, *A Low Energy Strategy for the UK*, International Institute for Environment and Development 1979.
Amory B. Lovins, *Soft Energy Paths*, Penguin 1977.
Alternative Technology: An answer to the energy crisis? Network of Alternative Technology and Technology Assessment, Open University 1980.

Useful periodicals

ATOM, monthly, United Kingdom Atomic Energy Authority, 11 Charles II Street, London SW1Y 4QP (Free).
The Bulletin of the Atomic Scientists, monthly, 10 Chesham Road, Amersham, Bucks HP6 5ES.
END Bulletin, quarterly, Bertrand Russell Peace Foundation Ltd, Bertrand Russell House, Gamble Street, Nottingham NG7 4ET.
Energy Bulletin, bi-monthly, Scottish Campaign to Resist the Atomic Menace (SCRAM), 30 Frederick Street, Edinburgh EH2 2JR.
New Statesman, weekly, 10 Great Turnstile, London WC1V 3DG.
Peace News, fortnightly, 8 Elm Avenue, Nottingham.
Sanity, bi-monthly, Campaign for Nuclear Disarmament, 11 Goodwin Street, London N4 3HQ.
WISE Bulletin, bi-monthly, World Information Service on Energy, 34 Cowley Road, Oxford.

References

1. The Birth of Siamese Twins pages 11-30

1. Margaret Gowing, *Britain and Atomic Energy 1939-1945*, Macmillan, 1964, p. 28. Much material in this chapter rests on the invaluable work done by the official atomic historian, Professor Margaret Gowing, and her assistant, Lorna Arnold, of the UKAEA. Responsibility for the arguments and conclusions, of course, rests with us.
2. Leslie Groves, *Now It Can Be Told*, Deutsch, 1963, p. 413.
3. Margaret Gowing, *op. cit.* p. 74.
4. Appendix to the Maud Report on 'Uranium as a source of power', contained in Margaret Gowing, *op. cit.* p. 435.
5. Margaret Gowing, *op. cit.* p. 161.
6. Uranium supply prospects were so poor at the time that there was concern about the rate at which the piles used it up. In order to keep the atomic reaction going in the piles, and hence create plutonium, it was necessary to keep adding fissile material. If uranium 235 were added to the uranium recovered from the spent fuel, rather than plutonium, it was obviously a more efficient method of producing plutonium.
7. 'Harwell's 21st Anniversary', lecture by Sir John Cockcroft reprinted in *ATOM*, no. 125, p. 51.
8. Margaret Gowing, *Independence and Deterrence Vol. 2, Policy Execution*, Macmillan, 1974, p. 299.
9. Gowing, in *Independence and Deterrence Vol. 1 Policy Making*, p. 213, draws attention to the severe lack of materials and services in post-war Britain, which only the project's high priority could circumvent. The Minister of Supply was quoted as saying that if the project had not been primarily for defence, it would not have got the steel needed for the plutonium piles.
10. Margaret Gowing, *Independence and Deterrence Vol. 1*, *op. cit.* p. 178.
11. This point was made in an exchange of letters between the Minister of Supply in 1947, G.R. Strauss, and Richard Crossman MP in the

New Statesman, 10 May 1963 to 7 June 1963, under the title 'Attlee and the bomb'. Strauss claimed there was no secrecy, and that Attlee could not prevent parliamentary debate – it was up to MPs to force one.

12. *House of Commons Debates*, 12 May 1948, column 2117.
13. Margaret Gowing, *Independence and Deterrence Vol. 1, op. cit.* p. 51.
14. *Ibid.* p. 406.
15. Senator MacMahon's bill was originally intended to provide a framework for US domestic control of atomic energy, to replace the earlier May-Johnson Bill, which atomic scientists had heavily criticised for giving too much control to the military. This contrasts with the acquiescence of British scientists over the total military domination of atomic energy.
16. Irwin Bupp and Jean-Claude Derian, *The Failed Promise of Nuclear Power*, Basic Books Inc., 1981, see Chapter 1, pp. 15-29.
17. J. Kay, *Britain's Atomic Factories*, HMSO, 1954. This book was the first publication on the atomic project, written to satisfy increasing demands by atomic scientists and politicians that the public be told something about the project.
18. Margaret Gowing, *Independence and Deterrence, Vol. 2, op. cit.* p. 293.
19. Margaret Gowing, *Independence and Deterrence, Vol. 1, op. cit.* p. 192.
20. *Ibid.* pp. 192-93.
21. Margaret Gowing, *Independence and Deterrence Vol. 2, op. cit.* p. 283.
22. Margaret Gowing, *Independence and Deterrence Vol. 1, op. cit.* p. 446.
23. *Ibid.* pp. 502-03.
24. Quoted in R.F. Pocock, *Nuclear Power: Its Development in the UK*, Allen and Unwin, 1978, pp. 36–37.
25. Leonard Beaton, 'Would Labour give up the bomb?', *Sunday Times* pamphlet, 1964, quoted in André Pierre, *Nuclear Politics*, Oxford University Press, 1972, p. 123.
26. *The Times*, 19 October 1957. The science correspondent wrote that the Calder Hall and Chapelcross reactors were approximately equivalent in terms of plutonium production to the Windscale piles. If we assume Gowing's figure of 15 bombs per year from one Windscale pile, then the four reactors at Calder Hall would be capable of producing enough plutonium for 60 bombs a year. Up to 1964, therefore, approximately 400 bombs could have been produced from this 'power station'.
27. Sir David Eccles, Minister of Works, *House of Commons Debates*, 10 December 1953.

28. Sir David Eccles, *House of Commons Debates*, 1 March 1954.
29. Quoted in R.F. Pocock, *Nuclear Power: Its Development in the UK, op. cit.* p. 40.
30. *First Annual Report*, UKAEA, 1954-55.
31. Margaret Gowing, *Independence and Deterrence, Vol. 2, op. cit.* p. 48.
32. *Sixth Annual Report*, UKAEA, 1959-60.
33. William Cook, the deputy director of Aldermaston at the UKAEA's inception was appointed UKAEA board member for engineering and production and then left in 1964 to become deputy scientific advisor at the Ministry of Defence. William Strath, UKAEA board member for external relations and commercial policy resigned in 1958 to become Permanent Secretary at the Ministry of Supply. J.R.V. Dolphin, chief engineer at Aldermaston, was later to be a prominent scientist at the National Radiological Protection Board. John Dunster started his career at Windscale's Research and Development division in 1950, moved through Health and Safety departments at Harwell and Risley, joined the Health and Safety Executive in 1976 and was transferred to head the National Radiological Protection Board in 1981. This information comes primarily from UKAEA Annual Reports, supported by volumes of *ATOM* and *Who's Who in Atoms*, Harrap Research Publications, 1969.
34. M.E. Webb, 'Some aspects of nuclear power economics in the UK', *Scottish Journal of Political Economy*, vol. xvi, 1968, p. 22, quoted in Roger Williams, *The Nuclear Power Decisions: British Policies 1953-78*, Croom Helm, 1980, p. 321.
35. Margaret Gowing, *Reflections on Atomic Energy History*, The Rede Lecture, Cambridge University Press, 1978, pp. 20-21.
36. Duncan Burn, *Nuclear Power and the Energy Crisis*, Macmillan, 1978, pp. 115-16.
37. *A Programme of Nuclear Power*, Cmnd. 93891, February 1955, p. 1.
38. Roger Williams, *The Nuclear Power Decisions, op. cit.* pp. 62-66.
39. Duncan Burn, *Nuclear Power and the Energy Crisis, op. cit.* p. 12. This book and Burn's previous one *The Political Economy of Nuclear Energy*, Institute of Economic Affairs, 1967, are a devastating attack on British nuclear decision-making and the economics of both Magnox and AGR programmes.
40. *The Nuclear Power Programme*, Cmnd. 1083, June 1960, p. 3.
41. See Walt Patterson, *Nuclear Power*, Penguin, 1980, pp. 162-66 for a fuller account of the accident.
42. *House of Commons Debates*, 24 June 1958, vol. 590, column 246 and 30 June 1958, vol. 590, column 857.
43. *House of Commons Debates*, 22 June 1959, vol. 607, column 849.

44. R.F. Pocock, *Nuclear Power: Its Development in the UK*, op. cit. p. 97.
45. Evidence that nuclear weapons can be made with higher proportions of plutonium 240 can be found in Albert Wohlstetter *et al*, *Swords from Ploughshares*, University of Chicago Press, 1979, pp. 39-42, and also Amory B. Lovins, 'Nuclear weapons and power-reactor plutonium', *Nature*, vol. 283, 1980, pp. 817-23.

    The plutonium in Magnox spent fuel is, in fact, potential weapons material without further purification. In a written parliamentary answer to Robin Cook MP on 29 October 1981, the Energy Secretary revealed that Magnox spent fuel contains 75 per cent plutonium 239.
46. *House of Commons Debates*, 24 June 1958, vol. 590, column 246-47.
47. 'The plutonium switch', *The Economist*, 21 June 1958, p. 1107.
48. R.F. Pocock, *Nuclear Power: Its Development in the UK*, op. cit. pp. 97-98.
49. Letter from Energy Under-Secretary David Mellor to Robin Cook MP, 18 December 1981.
50. *Seventh Annual Report*, UKAEA, 1960-61, p. 57.
51. *Ninth Annual Report*, UKAEA, 1962-63, p. 63.
52. *Eleventh Annual Report*, UKAEA, 1964-65, p. 16.
53. *Statement on Defence*, Cmnd. 2270, June 1964, para. 28.
54. *Ninth Annual Report*, UKAEA, 1962-63, p. 26.
55. *Statement on Defence*, op. cit. para. 29.
56. Private communication from James Daglish, PRO for the UKAEA, 29 September 1981.
57. Obtained from the figures for payments given in subsequent UKAEA Annual Reports and adjusting them using the Retail Price Index for the relevant years.
58. The best account can be found in Duncan Burn, *Nuclear Power and the Energy Crisis*, op. cit.
59. Martin Stott and Peter Taylor, *The Nuclear Controversy*, The Town and Country Planning Association in association with the Political Ecology Research Group, 1980, p. 11.
60. Duncan Burn, *Nuclear Power and the Energy Crisis*, op. cit. pp. 140-41.
61. David Henderson, 'Two British errors: their probable size and some possible lessons', Inaugural lecture, University College, London, Oxford Economic Papers, 1977.
62. Duncan Burn, Evidence to the House of Commons Select Committee on Energy, Vol. IV, 1981. pp. 1252-58.
63. Roger Williams, op. cit. pp. 325–26.
64. *Fifth Annual Report and Accounts*, BNFL, 1975-76, p. 19.
65. *House of Lords Debate*, 14 and 23 April 1970, quoted in *ATOM*, no.

164, June 1970. It may also be relevant here that government defence expenditure on 'special materials' (fissile material for nuclear weapons and submarine propulsion), which between 1965 and 1972 totalled £244 million (at current prices), ceased to be published separately after 1972. (Lawrence Freedman, *Britain and Nuclear Weapons*, Macmillan, Appendix 3, 1980, p. 144.)
66. Atomic Energy Authority (Weapons Group) Act, March 1973.

2. The Nuclear Chain pages 31-54

1. Duncan Campbell, 'World War III: an exclusive preview', *New Statesman*, 3 October 1980. We have not considered the role of nuclear plants as military targets in depth, partly because it is a peripheral issue and partly because it is well described elsewhere. See for example *Civilian Protection and Britain's Commercial Nuclear Installations*, the Political Ecology Research Group, published by The Ecology Party, 1981, and Bennett Ramberg, *Destruction of Nuclear Energy Facilities in War*, Lexington Books, D.C. Heath and Company, Toronto, 1980.
2. Margaret Gowing, *Independence and Deterrence*, Vol. 1, Macmillan, 1974, p. 168.
3. *Annual Report No. 9 1962-63*, UKAEA, para. 26.
4. Private communication from D.G. Avery, Deputy Managing Director, BNFL, to Robin Cook MP, 13 August 1981.
5. Martin Stott and Peter Taylor, *The Nuclear Controversy: A guide to the issues of the Windscale Inquiry*, The Town and Country Planning Association in association with the Political Ecology Research Group, 1980, p. 100.
6. *Ibid.* p. 101 and Duncan Campbell, 'Dangers of the Nuclear Convoys', *New Statesman*, 10 April 1981.
7. Parliamentary written answer to Robin Cook MP, 16 July 1981.
8. Quoted in Duncan Campbell, 'The Wings of the Green Parrot', *New Statesman*, 17 April 1981.
9. See parliamentary written answers to Gordon Wilson MP on 9 December 1980 and to Robin Cook MP on 16 July 1981.
10. *Annual Report*, UKAEA *op. cit.* para. 18.
11. See parliamentary written answers to Robin Cook MP on 16 February 1981 and 29 October 1981 and to Trevor Skeet MP on 4 March 1981.
12. Private communication from BNFL *op. cit.*
13. 'They'll carry H-Bomb rods', *Daily Record*, 2 May 1959.
14. *Chapelcross*, BNFL, 1980.
15. Ministry of Defence News Release, 27 April 1976.

16. Private communication from Fred Mulley, Secretary of State for Defence, to Mrs Helen Liddell, Secretary of the Labour Party in Scotland, 20 July 1981.
17. Parliamentary written answer to Robin Cook MP, 16 July 1981.
18. Private communication from Fred Mulley *op. cit.*
19. John Simpson, 'The Anglo-American Nuclear Relationship and its Implications for the Choice of a Possible Successor to the Current Polaris Force', evidence contained in Appendix 6 of *The Future of the United Kingdom's Nuclear Weapons Policy*, Sixth Report from the Expenditure Committee, Session 1978-79, 3 April 1979, p. 228, and David Fishlock, 'The Plutonium Hot Potato', *Financial Times*, 27 October 1981.
20. *Tenth Annual Reports and Accounts 1980-81*, BNFL, July 1981.
21. Ted Greenwood, George W. Rathjens and Jack Ruina, *Nuclear Power and Weapons Proliferation*, the International Institute for Strategic Studies, Adelphi Paper no. 130, 1976, pp. 22-25.
22. Leonard Beaton, 'Controlling the atom menace', *The Times*, 23 January 1969: see also C.F. Barnaby, 'The Gas Centrifuge Project', *Science Journal*, August 1967.
23. *Nuclear Engineering International*, April 1980.
24. *Tenth Annual Report*, BNFL *op. cit.*
25. *Nuclear Engineering International*, April 1981.
26. Parliamentary written answer from Mr Pym on 15 January 1980.
27. *Tenth Annual Report*, BNFL, *op. cit.* There were unconfirmed reports that the plant was at risk of being cancelled. See David Fishlock, 'Energy Department fights to save uranium project', *Financial Times*, 8 September 1981.
28. Norman Dombey, 'Fuelling suspicion', *The Guardian*, 3 December 1981. The original source is a US magazine *Nuclear Fuel*, 13 April 1981, p. 9.
29. Ted Greenwood *et al. op. cit.* p. 10 and *Nuclear Proliferation Factbook*, Environment and Natural Resources Policy Division, Congressional Research Service, Library of Congress, USA, September 1980, p. 175.
30. Henry Stanhope, 'Britain will produce arms-grade uranium', *The Times*, 10 January 1980.
31. Zdenek Cervenka and Barbara Rogers, *The Nuclear Axis*, Julian Friedmann, 1978, p. 308.
32. Simpson *op. cit.* p. 228.
33. *First Annual Report* 1955-56, UKAEA.
34. Parliamentary written answer to Robin Cook MP, 31 July 1981.
35. *Ibid.*
36. *Ibid.*
37. *Dumping at Sea*, Campaign Against Sea Dumping, Bath, 1981.

38. Private correspondence between Harwell and the naval dockyards, 25 June 1980, obtained by Greenpeace Ltd.
39. *Sixth Annual Report 1959-60*, UKAEA, p. 187.
40. *Memorandum submitted by Rolls Royce and Associates Limited* to the First Report from the House of Commons Select Committee on Energy, 13 February 1981, vol. II pp. 223-33.
41. Rob Edwards, 'New reactor for the ministry', *New Statesman*, 6 February 1981.
42. *Memorandum submitted by Rolls Royce and Associates Limited, op. cit.*
43. *Sixth Annual Report 1959-60*, UKAEA, p. 187, and *Annual Report 1977-78*, UKAEA, p. 22.
44. Parliamentary written answer to Robin Cook MP, 16 July 1981.
45. *Annual Report 1980-81*, UKAEA.
46. Amory B. Lovins, 'Nuclear weapons and power-reactor plutonium', *Nature*, vol. 283, 28 February 1980, pp. 817-23, vol. 284, 13 March 1980, p. 190, and Ted Greenwood *et al*, *op. cit.* p. 3. The critical mass of plutonium 239 – the minimum amount necessary to sustain a chain reaction above which supercriticality (i.e. an explosion) occurs – is about ten kilogrammes. But this can be dramatically reduced by surrounding the plutonium with a material that reflects neutrons. Extremely high compression enables the critical mass to be reduced to under two kilogrammes.
47. Parliamentary written answer to Robin Cook MP, 15 April 1981.
48. *The transport of plutonium in the form of nitrate solution between Dounreay and Windscale*, Health and Safety Executive, 1979, p. 6.
49. Lovins *op. cit.*
50. *Nuclear Power and the Environment*, Royal Commission on Environmental Pollution, Sixth Report, Chairman Sir Brian Flowers, Cmnd. 6618, 1976, p. 202.
51. 'What Future for the "Breeder"', *ATOM* 297, July 1981, p. 182.
52. *Materials Unaccounted For – 1980*, UKAEA Press Release, 12 December 1980.
53. *Ibid.* Also UKAEA Press Releases of 31 October 1979, 7 November 1978 and 21 June 1977.
54. Ministry of Defence job advertisement in *New Scientist*, 30 October 1981.
55. Anthony Tucker, 'Rebuilding Programme Planned at Aldermaston Nuclear Plant', *The Guardian*, 20 December 1980.
56. *AWRE: Atomic Weapons Research Establishment*, Ministry of Defence Public Relations and the Central Office of Information, undated, p. 5.
57. Parliamentary written answer to Robin Cook MP, 16 July 1981.

58. Walter C. Patterson, *Nuclear Power*, Penguin, 1980, p. 90.
59. R.M.Fry, *Radiation Hazards of Uranium Mining and Milling*, Australian Atomic Energy Commission Report IP9, 1975.
60. Alun Roberts, *The Rössing File*, Campaign Against the Namibian Uranium Contract, 1980.
61. *Ibid.* p. 8.
62. Letter to *The Guardian*, 13 September 1973.
63. Parliamentary written answer from Francis Pym MP, 18 February 1980.
64. Cervenka and Rogers *op. cit.* p. 308.
65. Royal Commission on Environmental Pollution *op. cit.* p. 95.
66. Rosalie Bertell, *Radiation and Species Survival*, unpublished paper, 1979, pp. 1-4.
67. Eliot Marshall, 'New A-bomb Studies Alter Radiation Estimates', *Science*, vol. 212, 22 May 1981, pp. 900-3 and Anthony Tucker, 'Atomic Bomb Research Suggests Greater Cancer Danger From Low-Level Radiation', *The Guardian*, 25 May 1981.
68. *Radiation: Your health at risk*, Radiation and Health Information Service, Cambridge, 1980.
69. 'Disease legacy from Nevada atomic tests', *New Scientist*, November 1979, pp. 336-38.
70. Evans, Buckton *et al.* 'Radiation-induced chromosome aberrations in nuclear dockyard workers', *Nature* 277, 15 February 1979, pp. 531-34.
71. Rob Edwards, 'Dockyards damage your health', *New Statesman*, 5 December 1980 and William Robertson, 'Expert confirms submen's atom fears', *Sunday Standard*, 28 June 1981.
72. Figures derived from *Nuclear Establishments 1975-76 and 1977-78*, Health and Safety Executive 1978 and 1979.
73. 'What Price Jobs', *SCRAM Energy Bulletin* no. 25, August/September 1981, p. 11.
74. Robin Cook MP asked three parliamentary written questions, two on 16 July 1981 and one on 24 July 1981, to try and discover the source of fissile material for Trident missiles, and the total amounts of plutonium produced for civil and military use. None of these questions was answered.
75. Based on *World Armaments: The Nuclear Threat*, Stockholm International Peace Research Institute, 1977, p. 22; Leonard Beaton, *Capabilities of Non-Nuclear Powers*, in *A World of Nuclear Powers*, Ed. Alistair Buchan, The American Assembly, Prentice Hall, Englewood Cliff, 1966, p. 15, and informed private sources.
76. See for example parliamentary written answer to Robin Cook MP on 24 July 1981.
77. John Nott, 'Decisions to modernise UK's nuclear contribution to

NATO strengthen deterrence', *NATO Review* vol. 29 no. 2, April 1981, pp. 1-5.
78. Duncan Campbell, 'The Wings of the Green Parrot', *New Statesman*, 17 April 1981.
79. Private communication from Energy Under Secretary John Moore to Robin Cook MP, 22 March 1982.
80. *Proposed amendments to the agreement for co-operation with the United Kingdom . . . on the uses of atomic energy for mutual defence purposes*, 15 July 1959, p. 12, quoted in Simpson *op. cit.* reference 19 above, and Norman Dombey *op. cit.*
81. Private communication from James Daglish, UKAEA, 29 September 1981.
82. *Amendment to the Agreement . . . for co-operation on the uses of atomic energy for mutual defence purposes of July 3, 1958*, July 1980, Cmnd. 7976.
83. *Hansard*, 21 April 1964, quoted in Norman Dombey *op. cit.*
84. 'US wants to buy British atom fuel', *The Guardian*, 12 October 1981. See also parliamentary written answer to Mr Mudd MP on 19 October 1981. Nuclear industry representatives have talked in terms of 'several tonnes'.
85. Thomas B. Cochran and Barbara Finamore, *Statement on behalf of The Natural Resources Defence Council before the Subcommittee on Oversight and Investigation of the House Committee on Interior and Insular Affairs on the Potential Use of American Spent Fuel to Produce Nuclear Weapons*, 1 October 1981, p. 10.
86. David Fishlock, 'IAEA aghast that America may turn to civilian reactor fuel for weapons production', *The Energy Daily*, Washington US, 28 September 1981.
87. R.V. Hesketh, letter to *The Times*, 30 October 1981.
88. Parliamentary written answer to Trevor Skeet MP on 3 March 1981.
89. According to a parliamentary written answer from Energy Under-Secretary Norman Lamont on 3 March 1980, advanced gas-cooled reactors and pressurised water reactors yield respectively 25 per cent and 44 per cent as much plutonium as Magnox reactors.

3. Atoms for Peace? pages 55-79

1. *Sunday Times*, 14 June 1981.
2. *The Times*, 9 June 1981.
3. *Ibid.*
4. *The Guardian*, 9 June 1981.
5. Interview with the head of the Pakistani nuclear programme, *New Scientist*, 11 July 1981, p. 690.

6. Margaret Gowing, *Independence and Deterrence*, Vol. 1, London, Macmillan, 1974, p. 88.
7. Fred Iklé, foreward to Albert Wohlstetter *et al*, *Swords from Ploughshares*, University of Chicago Press, 1979, p. x.
8. Address by Dwight D. Eisenhower, US President, to the United Nations General Assembly on 8 December 1953.
9. Amory B. Lovins, 'Nuclear weapons and nuclear power production', *Nature*, vol. 283, 1980, pp. 817-23.
10. Albert Wohlstetter, Evidence to Windscale Inquiry, Day 58, 1977, pp. 36-37.
11. Amory B. Lovins and L. Hunter Lovins, *Energy/War: Breaking the nuclear link*, San Francisco, Friends of the Earth, 1981, p. 19.
12. John Foster Dulles, quoted in Robert Jungk, *The Nuclear State*, John Calder, 1979, p. 92.
13. Report of the Secretary-General of the United Nations, *Nuclear Weapons*, London, Francis Pinter, 1981, pp. 23-25.
14. *Swords from Ploughshares*, op. cit. p. 1.
15. 'A report on the international control of atomic energy', US State Department, 2498, 16 March 1946.
16. *Swords from Ploughshares*, op. cit. p. 50.
17. *Financial Times*, 30 July 1981.
18. Ted Greenwood, George W. Rathjens and Jack Ruina, *Nuclear power and nuclear weapons proliferation*, International Institute for Strategic Studies, Adelphi Paper no. 130, 1976, p. 3.
19. Elaine Davenport, Paul Eddy and Peter Gillman, *The Plumbat Affair*, London, Futura, 1978, chapter 19, pp. 160-70.
20. *Financial Times*, 30 July 1981.
21. IAEA Annual Report for 1981, summarised in *ATOM*, no. 300. October 1981, p. 271.
22. *Newsweek*, 22 July 1981, p. 18.
23. 'Congress stirs non-proliferation row', *Nature*, vol. 292, 9 July 1981, p. 99.
24. *Financial Times*, 13 July 1981.
25. Special Safeguards Implementation Report, IAEA, GOV/1842, 8 June 1977, quoted in Zdenek Cervenka and Barbara Rogers, *The Nuclear Axis*, London, Friedmann Books, 1978, p. 205.
26. *The Scotsman*, 10 June 1981.
27. *World Armaments and Disarmament*, SIPRI Yearbook 1981, London, Taylor and Francis Ltd, 1981, p. xviii.
28. Frank Barnaby, 'On the second NPT review conference', *Bulletin of the Atomic Scientists*, vol. 36, no. 7, September 1980, p. 20.
29. 'Black Africa states urged to join nuclear league', *The Guardian*, 13 December 1979.

30. Report of the Secretary-General of the United Nations, *Nuclear Weapons, op. cit.* pp. 175-79.
31. Nuclear Energy Policy Study Group, *Nuclear Power: Issues and Choices*, (sponsored by the Ford Foundation and administered by the MITRE Corporation), Cambridge MA, Ballinger, 1977.
32. *Statement of Thomas B. Cochrane and Barbara A. Finamore on behalf of the Natural Resources Defence Council Inc., before the Sub-committee on Oversight and Investigation of the House Committee on Interior and Insular Affairs on the Potential use of American commercial spent fuel to produce nuclear weapons*, 1 October 1981.
33. *Washington Post*, 16 February 1977.
34. Sverre Lodgaard, 'International nuclear commerce', *Bulletin of Peace Proposals*, vol. 8, no. 1, 1977, p. 23.
35. Dan Smith, *South Africa's Nuclear Capability*, World Campaign against Military and Nuclear Collaboration with South Africa, February 1980, p. 7.
36. Dan Smith, *ibid*, p. 24.
37. Dr P.M.S. Jones, *ATOM*, no. 291, January 1981, p. 23.
38. Victor Gilinsky, paper presented to the British Nuclear Forum Fuel Cycle Conference, London, September 1978.
39. Duncan Burn, House of Commons Select Committee on Energy Memorandum, vol. IV, 1981, p. 1253.
40. Robert Alvarez, statement to the House Science and Technology sub-committee on Nuclear and Fossil Fuel Research and Development, March 1977, quoted in *The Nuclear Axis, op. cit.* p. 291.
41. *The Guardian*, 22 October 1981.
42. *The Nuclear Axis, op. cit.* p. 292.
43. *The Nuclear State, op. cit.* p. 76.
44. *The Nuclear Axis, op. cit.* p. 294.
45. *The Plumbat Affair, op. cit.* which has a general account of Israel's nuclear activities.
46. *Financial Times*, 14 April 1981.
47. Andrew McKillop, 'Oil: the energy dilemma', in *Nuclear Links*, Third World First/Students Against Nuclear Energy, 1981, p. 6.
48. *Energy in Developing Countries*, World Bank, 1980.
49. McKillop, *op. cit.* p. 7.
50. *Swords from Ploughshares, op. cit.* p. 77.
51. Walter Marshall, 'Nuclear power and the proliferation issue', *ATOM*, no. 258, April 1978, pp. 78-102.
52. *Energy/War: Breaking the nuclear link, op. cit.* p. 28.
53. *Time*, 9 July 1979, pp. 32-33.
54. Walter Marshall, *op. cit.*
55. *Energy/War: Breaking the nuclear link, op. cit.* p. 15.

4. Towards the Nuclear State pages 80-97

1. Peter Goodchild, *J. Robert Oppenheimer: 'Shatterer of Worlds'*, BBC 1981, on which the preceding account is based.
2. The case of Karen Silkwood has been described in greater detail elsewhere. See for example Howard Kohn, 'Malignant Giant: the nuclear industry's terrible power and how it silenced Karen Silkwood', in *Rolling Stone*, New York, 27 March 1975; Jim Garrison, *From Hiroshima to Harrisburg: The Unholy Alliance*, SCM Press, 1980, pp. 208-23; and Peter Bunyard, *Nuclear Britain*, New English Library, 1981, pp. 203-06.
3. Edward Pochin, *Report of an Investigation into Radiological Health and Safety at the Ministry of Defence (Procurement Executive) Atomic Weapons Research Establishment Aldermaston*, Harwell, 30 October 1978.
4. David Loshak, 'Safety fears stall Britain's A-weapon programme', *NOW*, 21 November 1980.
5. We are very grateful for the help of Trevor Brown in compiling this account.
6. Margaret Gowing, *Reflections on Atomic Energy History*, The Rede Lecture, Cambridge University Press, 1978.
7. Roger Williams, *The Nuclear Power Decisions: British Policies 1953-78*, Croom Helm, 1980.
8. Parliamentary written answer to Robin Cook MP on 15 April 1981. The other parliamentary answers referred to were on 15 April 1981 and 10 July 1981. There are many similar examples that could be quoted.
9. Cabinet committee minutes printed as Appendix 8 in *Poison in our Hills*, Scottish Campaign to Resist the Atomic Menace, 1980, p. 63.
10. *Hansard*, 1 March 1954.
11. Sir John Hill, 'The Abuse of Nuclear Power', *ATOM* 239, September 1976, p. 4.
12. Much of this information is contained in a parliamentary written answer to Jo Richardson MP on 27 April 1981.
13. See for example the seminal study, Michael Flood and Robin Grove-White, *Nuclear Prospects: A comment on the Individual, the State and Nuclear Power*, Friends of the Earth in association with the National Council for Civil Liberties and The Council for the Protection of Rural England, October 1976, and Robert Jungk, *The Nuclear State*, John Calder, 1979.
14. Royal Commission on Environmental Pollution Sixth Report, *Nuclear Power and the Environment*, Chairman Sir Brian Flowers, Cmnd. 6618, 1976, p. 129.
15. Flood and Grove-White, *op. cit.*

16. Brian Sedgemore, *The Secret Constitution: an Analysis of the Political Establishment*, Hodder and Stoughton, 1980, p. 126.
17. *Ibid.* pp. 98-104.
18. David Elliott *et al. The Politics of Nuclear Power*, Pluto Press, 1978.
19. Eric Fletcher MP on 1 March 1954, in *Hansard*.
20. Williams, *op. cit.* p. 25.
21. Emrys Hughes MP on 29 April 1954, in *Hansard*.
22. Sir Christopher Hinton, 'Two Decades of Nuclear Confusion', *New Scientist*, 28 October 1976, p. 200.
23. First Report from the Select Committee on Energy, *The Government's Statement on the New Nuclear Power Programme*, February 1981, vol. 1, pp. 70-73.
24. Sedgemore, *op. cit.* p. 107.
25. *Ibid.* pp. 108-25. See also *Memorandum submitted by The Rt Hon Tony Benn MP* to the Select Committee on energy *op. cit.* vol. 2, pp. 394-95.
26. Tony Benn, *Arguments for Socialism*, Penguin, 1980, p. 81.
27. David Dickson, *Alternative Technology and the Politics of Technical Change*, Futura, 1974.
28. Margaret Gowing, *Independence and Deterrence*, Vol. 1, Macmillan, 1974, p. 234.
29. John Simpson, *Strategic Nuclear Weapons Policy*, evidence to House of Commons Defence Committee, 20 May 1981.
30. Stuart Hall, 'Missiles, Reactors and Civil Liberties', in *Missiles, Reactors and Civil Liberties: Against the Nuclear State*, Scottish Council for Civil Liberties, 1981.
31. E.P. Thompson, 'The State of the Nation', in *Writing by Candlelight*, Merlin Press, 1980. A classic example of state manipulation of the media occurred in 1981 when E.P. Thompson himself was barred from delivering the BBC Dimbleby Lecture on the subject of the nuclear arms race.
32. E.P. Thompson, *Protest and Survive*, Penguin, 1980; 'Freedom and the Bomb', in *New Statesman*, 24 April 1981; and 'Can Europe Halt the next World War?', in *The Sunday Times*, 9 August 1981.
33. Walter C. Patterson, *The Fissile Society*, Earth Resources Research, 1977.
34. Jungk, *op. cit.* p. 45.
35. Ivan Illich, *Tools for Conviviality*, Fontana, 1975.

5. Breaking the Nuclear Chain pages 98-105

1. Quoted in Ronald W. Clark, *The Greatest Power on Earth: The Story of Nuclear Fission*, Sidgwick and Jackson, 1980, p. 288.

2. For a full analysis of non-nuclear energy strategies see Amory Lovins, *Soft Energy Paths*, Penguin, 1977; Gerald Leach *et al. A Low Energy Strategy for the UK*, International Institute for Environment and Development, 1979; and *Alternative Technology – An Answer to the Energy Crisis?*, Network for Alternative Technology and Technology Assessment, Open University, 1980.
3. Kevin P. Donnelly, *The Department of Energy's Forecasting Methodology: A Critique*, Glasgow Friends of the Earth, 1981.
4. See for example J.W. Jeffrey, 'The real costs of nuclear power in the UK', in *Energy Policy*, December 1980, and *Cheap Electrickery: The Real Cost of Nuclear Power in Scotland*, Scottish Consumer Campaign Against Nuclear Power, 1981.
5. The Monopolies and Mergers Commission, *Central Electricity Generating Board*, May 1981, p. 292.
6. Cabinet committee minutes printed as Appendix 8 in *Poison in our Hills*, Scottish Campaign to Resist the Atomic Menace, 1980, p. 63.
7. Martin Dickson, 'Regenerating the nuclear option', *Financial Times*, 4 February 1981.
8. First Report from the Select Committee on Energy, *The Government's Statement on the new nuclear power programme*, February 1981, vol. 1, p. 63.
9. *Ibid.* p. 55.
10. *Towards a Sustainable Energy Policy*, memorandum submitted by Friends of the Earth in *ibid.* vol. 2, p. 524.
11. See table in Robin Cook, *No Nukes*, Fabian Tract 475, July 1981, p. 15.
12. Leach *op. cit.*
13. Select Committee on Energy, *op. cit.* vol. 1, p. 26.
14. Friends of the Earth *op. cit.* p. 526.
15. *Ibid.*
16. Michael Flood *et al. The Pressurised Water Reactor: A critique of the Government's Nuclear Power Programme*, Friends of the Earth Energy Paper no. 4, 1981, pp. 43-50.
17. Sir John Hill, 'The Driving Forces of Proliferation', *ATOM* 274, August 1979, p. 201.
18. Quoted in William Robertson, 'A cover-up at Windscale?', *Sunday Standard*, 25 October 1981.
19. This observation is made in Amory B. Lovins and L. Hunter Lovins, *Energy/War: Breaking the Nuclear Link*, Friends of the Earth, San Francisco, 1981, p. 3.

Index

Advanced gas-cooled reactors 17,33,34,39, 54,93,101
    costs 28,73
Aldermaston 14,15-16,18,27,30,40,41, 43-44,87,104,108
    health and safety 82-84
American weapons connection 52-53
Anderson, Sir John 13,14,21,85
Atoms for Peace 58-61,71,72
Atomic Bomb Casualty Commission 47

Brazil 38,56,66,70,73,76,78
British Nuclear Fuels Ltd 31,33,34,36,38,39, 46,89,93
    military subsidy 29
    health and safety 48-49
Brown, Trevor 82-84,88,96

Calder Hall 20,27,29,35,39,48,49,52
    plutonium production 21,51,109
Capenhurst 13,15,17,23,27,29,36-39,51,52, 89,95,104
    and H-bombs 37,49
    submarine fuel 38
Campaign for Nuclear Disarmament 98,99, 100
Central Electricity Generating Board 22,23, 24,26,41,53,92,98,101
Chapelcross 20,27,29,35-36,48,49,52,89,95
    plutonium production 27,51,109
    tritium plant 36
Civil liberties 76,81,88-91,95-96
Cockcroft, John 15,17,22
Combined heat and power 92,102

Dounreay 33,40-43,87,89
    MUF 43
Dungeness B 28

Energy
    and the Third World 74-76
    coal 19,24
    conservation 102
    oil 24
    renewable 103
Enrichment 13,61,73,78,104,107
    gas diffusion 14,37
    weapons-grade and civil 37
    plant in non-weapons states 70 (Table 2)
    centrifuge 37,38
Euratom 44,63

Fast breeder reactor 19,23,24,25,42,53,54, 108
    and proliferation 42-43,77-78
France 45, 62,72
    and NPT 66,74
    and Iraq 56-57,74
    and Pakistan 74

Gowing, Margaret 16,18,19,20,22,23,85,86, 88,94

Harwell 14,15,16,18,19,40,47,89
Hill, Sir John 21,38,87,89,90,103
Hinkley Point 28
    military modification 26-27
Hinton, Christopher 15,17,22,24,85,92
HMS Vulcan 40-41,95

ICI 12
India 66,68,69,70,78
International Atomic Energy Agency 53,57, 58,62-65,66,70,73
International Commission on Radiological Protection 46
International Fuel Cycle Evaluation 77
Iraq 55
    nuclear programme 56-57
Israel 55,56,57,64,66,70,74

Lilienthal-Acheson Report 58,62
Light water reactors 17 (see PWR)
Low-level radiation 46-49

MacMahon Act 17,26
Magnox reactors 17,23,24,25,28,35,39
    economics 23-24
    military modification 26-27
    plutonium production 51,52,54,109
Manhattan Project 13,15,61,73,80
Marshall, Walter 77-79,92
Material Unaccounted For (MUF) 43,63
Maud Committee 12,13
Ministry of Defence 25,27,30,31,34,36,37, 39,41,43,44,48,49,52,54

National Radiological Protection Board 46-47,48,83
NATO 9,51,90
Non-Proliferation Treaty 55,57,58,64, 65-69,70,72,73
    articles of 65 (Table 2)
    and disarmament 66-69

Nuclear free zones 105
Nuclear Installations Inspectorate 89
Nuclear power
   consortia 23
   and disarmament 103-105
   economics 19,24,28,73,102
   employment 94,102
   need 100-101
   orders for 101
   overcapacity 101
   reactors in non-weapons states 67 (Table 3)
   secrecy 23,81,87,88
   trade unions 91,100,101
   UK programmes 9,22,23,24-25,93
Nuclear Suppliers Group 69
Nuclear submarines
   Capenhurst 37,38
   fuel enrichment 38
   Polaris 9,34,51,68,94
   spent fuel storage 34
   Trident 9,34,41,44,68,87,94,95,98,100,104
   US-UK Agreement on fuel 37,52
Nuclear waste 90,105,108
   ocean dumping 40
Nuclear weapons
   Cruise 9,68,95,100,104
   fissile material composition 42,49
   fission bombs 35,49
   H-bombs 27,36,37,81,106
   lifespan 34
   reprocessing 33-34
   secrecy 13,16-17,85
   UK programme 9,14,36,51,54
   US programme 53

Operation Square Leg 31
Oppenheimer, J. Robert 13,80-82,88,96
Osirak 55,56,63,64,66,70

Pakistan 37,66,78
Penney, William 15,17,22,85
PIPPA 19
Plutonium
   nitrate 41-42,87,89
   reactor- vs weapons-grade 26,60-61,107
   plutonium credit 24
   under IAEA safeguards 63
   US-UK swop 52-53
Pressurised water reactor 41,54,90,93
Proliferation
   and nuclear power 60-61,69,73,74,76,77,79,98,104
   and research reactors 59 (Table 1),61
   US policy 34,52,70-71,73

ROF Burghfield 43,104,108
Reprocessing 13,27,61,78,104,107
   plants in non-weapons states 70 (Table 4)
   by laser 53
Rolls Royce and Associates 40-41
Rössing contract 44-46,88
Rosyth 34,40,48
RTZ 44-46,88

Secrecy 13,16-17,23,31,49,81,84-88
   health and safety 48,82
   classified information 86-88,89,101
   trade union rights 91
   IAEA 64
Silkwood, Karen 82,88,96
Simpson, John 39,95
Sizewell 9,41
South Africa 44,45,46,70,71-73,76
Springfields 15,17,23,29,39,89,104

Thompson, E. P. 95-96
Three Mile Island 93,100
Torness 90,93,98,100,103
Trident see Nuclear submarines
Tritium 36,49,52,95,108

United Kingdom Atomic Energy Authority 21,25,33,34,39,40,41,42,43,44,46,52,77,85,87,88,91-93
   military personnel 22
   military subsidy 21-22,27-28
   policy-making role 28-29,92
   Weapons Group 29-30
   Special Constables 42,89
   Rössing contract 45
   employees 22,27,89
Uranium mining 44-46,71, 106-107
UK-US Defence Agreement 36,37,52
URENCO 37-38

Windscale 15,17,18,23,27,29,31-35,39,42,49,54,87,104
   1957 accident 25
   Windscale Inquiry 33,34,90
   warhead reprocessing 33-34
   MUF 43
   security 89
   plutonium emissions 33
   plutonium fuel fabrication 33
   radiation exposure 33,48-49

Anti-Nuclear Organisations in Britain

Anti-Nuclear Campaign (ANC)
P.O. Box 216
Sheffield S1 1BD
Telephone: 0742-754691

Campaign for Nuclear Disarmament (CND)
11 Goodwin Street
London N4 3HQ
Telephone: 01-263 4954

European Nuclear Disarmament (END)
227 Seven Sisters Road
London N4
Telephone: 01-380 0532

Friends of the Earth (FoE)
9 Poland Street
London W1V 3DG
Telephone: 01-434 1684

The Scottish Campaign to Resist the Atomic Menace (SCRAM)
30 Frederick Street
Edinburgh EH2 2JR
Telephone: 031-225 7752

Socialist Environment and Resources Association (SERA)
9 Poland Street
London W1V 3DG
Telephone: 01-349 3749